The Black Arc

DARK WATER / DEATH IN HEAVEN

By Philip Purser-Hallard

Published March 2016 by Obverse Books

Cover Design © Cody Schell
Text © Philip Purser-Hallard, 2016

Range Editors: Stuart Douglas, Philip Purser-Hallard

Philip would like to thank:

*Stuart Douglas at Obverse Books, for encouraging the **Black Archive** project from the start, and to the growing number of authors who have agreed to contribute to it; my ever-tolerant family for allowing me the time to write this book and edit the others in the series; everyone who read and commented on the manuscript, especially Jon Arnold and Alan Stevens; and Steven Moffat and all the creators of Doctor Who ancient and modern, for providing such an endlessly fascinating subject of investigation for us all.*

To Rachel Churcher, who might enjoy it

4

CONTENTS

Overview

Synopsis

Introduction: 'So, What's Happened?'

Chapter 1. 'Everyone in London Just Clapped': The Season Finale

Chapter 2. 'I've Been Up and Down Your Timeline': Gathering the Threads

Chapter 3. 'The Army of the Dead': The Seasonal Special

Chapter 4. 'Queen of Evil': Trans-figuring the Master

Chapter 5. 'How May I Assist You with Your Death?': Death and What Comes After

Chapter 6. 'Cybermen from Cyberspace': Is This Cyberpunk?

Conclusion: 'So, What Now?'

Appendix: 'You Can See My House from Here'

Bibliography

Biography

OVERVIEW

Serial Title: *Dark Water / Death in Heaven*

Writer: Steven Moffat

Director: Rachel Talalay

Original UK Transmission Dates: 1 November 2014 – 8 November 2014

Running Time: *Dark Water* 46m 29s

                     Death in Heaven: 57m 9s

UK Viewing Figures: *Dark Water* 7.34 million

                     Death in Heaven: 7.6 million

Regular cast: Peter Capaldi (The Doctor), Jenna Coleman (Clara)

Recurring Cast: Samuel Anderson (Danny), Michelle Gomez (Missy), Ingrid Oliver (Osgood), Jemma Redgrave (Kate Lethbridge-Stewart)

Guest Cast: Joan Blackham (Woman), Sheila Reid (Gran), Chris Addison (Seb), Andrew Leung (Dr Chang), Bradley Ford (Fleming), Antonio Bourouphael (Boy), Nigel Betts (Mr Armitage), Sanjeev Bhaskar (Colonel Ahmed), Shane Keogh-Grenade (Teenage Boy), Katie Bignell (Teenage Girl), James Pearse (Graham), Jeremiah Krage (Cyberman), Nicholas Briggs (Voice of the Cybermen), Nick Frost (Santa Claus)

Antagonists: Missy, the Cybermen

Sequels and Prequels: *Last Christmas* (2014), *The Magician's Apprentice / The Witch's Familiar* (2015)

6

Responses:

'This finale couldn't lift itself up from the messy morass of the rest of the season... it didn't make sense, it was ridiculous and contrived and just not engaging.'

[Gavin Clarke, 'Doctor Who Trashing the TARDIS, Clara Alone, Useless UNIT: Death in Heaven'. *The Register*, 8 November 2014]

'Steven Moffat has concluded a startling creative resurgence for the show with a finale that typifies what has made all of season eight so successful. *Death In Heaven* is ambitious, and it sometimes throws around more ideas than it knows what to do with, but it succeeds because it hits the right balance between plot and character, between the mythos and the human story.'

[Alasdair Wilkins, 'Doctor Who: Death in Heaven'. AV Club, 8 November 2014]

SYNOPSIS

Dark Water

After **Clara**'s boyfriend **Danny** is killed in a car accident, she tries to blackmail **the Doctor** into changing the past. Instead he offers to take her to search for Danny in whatever afterlife may exist.

Their search takes them to a mausoleum run by an organisation called 3W, where skeletal bodies are preserved in tanks of 'dark water', a fluid which conceals non-organic structures. They meet **Missy**, a mysterious woman in black who has been seen in earlier stories greeting the souls of the recently dead, although she now claims to be a robot receptionist.

Meanwhile Danny is inducted into the afterlife, known as the Nethersphere, by Missy's assistant **Seb**. Seb introduces him to another of the dead, **a young boy** whom Danny accidentally killed while serving in the army.

3W's **Dr Chang** explains to the Doctor and Clara why the organisation offers its service: its founder discovered that the dead continue to feel what is done to their bodies, and that cremation is an appalling agony to them. Chang and Seb enable a conversation between Clara and Danny, but Danny fears that Clara will try to join him in the Nethersphere by dying, so refuses to prove his identity to her. After she cuts him off, Seb offers Danny the opportunity to 'delete' his troubling emotions.

Meanwhile, Missy – a Time Lord who has created the Nethersphere using Gallifreyan technology – begins to revive 3W's entombed dead. She is reuniting the uploaded and modified minds she has collected with their upgraded bodies, now revealed as **Cybermen**.

9

The Doctor discovers that the 3W facility is located inside St Paul's Cathedral. As Cybermen emerge onto the streets of London, Missy announces herself as the Mistress, the Time Lord villain formerly known as 'the Master'.

Death in Heaven

Across the world, Cybermen at 3W facilities are activated, then launch themselves on rocket boots into the sky, where they explode, creating global cloud cover. The clouds begin to rain on dead people, chiefly in graveyards, and shortly they start to rise as Cybermen. One of these is Danny, physically converted but still in possession of his emotions, who rescues Clara from the mausoleum.

The Time Lords are kidnapped by UNIT, led by **Kate Stewart** and her assistant **Osgood**, and taken aboard a plane which falls under attack by flying Cybermen. Osgood is killed by Missy, and Kate is sucked out into the atmosphere. The Doctor manages to escape and joins Clara and Danny in a graveyard, where he and Clara manually disable Danny's emotions, to relieve his distress at his condition.

Missy plans to convert the living as well as the dead, creating a Cyber-army – which is, she explains when she joins them, her birthday present for the Doctor. She wants to help him enforce his high ideals across the cosmos; she wants her friend back.

The Doctor, who since his regeneration has been beset by doubts as to whether he is 'a good man', hands control of the Cyber-army to Danny, who remains committed to protecting Clara. At Danny's command, the converted dead launch themselves into the sky and blow themselves up, ending the threat from the cloud.

Missy tempts the Doctor with the whereabouts of Gallifrey, but Clara persuades him to kill her to prevent further suffering. Before he can do so, Missy is apparently vaporised by a Cyberman who has rescued Kate from falling to her death, and would seem to be Kate's father, the late **Brigadier Lethbridge-Stewart**.

Two weeks later, Danny manages to open a temporary pathway from the collapsing Nethersphere to Clara's flat. Instead of resurrecting himself, he returns the boy he killed, asking Clara to take care of him. Meanwhile, the Doctor finds only empty space at the co-ordinates Missy gave for Gallifrey.

Meeting in a café, the Doctor and Clara lie to one another, pretending that Danny and Gallifrey have been restored to them and that all is well. After they go their separate ways, **Santa Claus** appears in the TARDIS and asks for the Doctor's Christmas wish list.

INTRODUCTION: 'SO, WHAT'S HAPPENED?'

Every new episode of **Doctor Who** has high expectations placed on it: as a source of frightening yet ultimately comforting stories for children; as diverting entertainment for British and global audiences of wildly disparate ages and backgrounds; as a sophisticated text, subject to merciless scrutiny by a worldwide community of critically engaged fans; as a showcase for the talent and professionalism of the BBC; and as the latest chapter in an odyssey through space, time and genre which has lasted over half a century and is the greatest sustained heroic epic Western television has produced.

An actor's first season in the part of the Doctor accentuates this pressure as the public acclimatise themselves to the idiosyncrasies of a new lead; and in 2014, Peter Capaldi's first year as the 12th Doctor brought the additional challenge of following 2013's 50th anniversary celebrations. These had seen a succession of special episodes[1] featuring a tour of the Doctor's personal history; a flashback to the first Doctor's departure from Gallifrey; new appearances in the role by former Doctors Tom Baker, Paul

---

[1] The full set of **Doctor Who** stories included in the 50th anniversary 'Collector's Edition' DVD set is: the season finale, *The Name of the Doctor*, the short webcast episodes 'The Night of the Doctor' and 'The Last Day', the anniversary special *The Day of the Doctor* and the Christmas special *The Time of the Doctor* (all 2013, for obvious reasons). The extensive additional material does not form part of the continuing **Doctor Who** narrative (despite a cameo from Matt Smith, in costume as the Doctor, in the historical docudrama *An Adventure in Space and Time*).

13

McGann and David Tennant; archive footage of all the other Doctors, some of them digitally manipulated to interact with the current cast; the casting of cinematic giant Sir John Hurt as a previously-unseen past incarnation; extensive footage of the cataclysmic Time War that forms the backdrop to the 21st-century series; a plethora of reappearing monsters from across the programme's history[2]; and the swansong of the incumbent Doctor Matt Smith; as well as Capaldi's own first appearances in the role, guesting as a pair of scowling eyebrows before his full-facial debut[3].

Because of the typical structure of 21st-century seasons of **Doctor Who**, the two-part finale *Dark Water / Death in Heaven* (2014) bore the second greatest burden of this weight, after Capaldi's first full episode as the Doctor, *Deep Breath* (2014). Steven Moffat, **Doctor Who**'s showrunner[4] who had written all the previous year's celebratory stories, scripted all three episodes, as well as writing or co-writing four others during the season[5].

---

[2] From the Daleks, introduced in 'The Dead Planet' (*The Daleks* episode 1, 1963) to the Silents, introduced in *The Impossible Astronaut* (2011).

[3] In *The Day of the Doctor* and *The Time of the Doctor* respectively.

[4] Moffat's official title is Executive Producer; he also refers to himself as 'head writer'. 'Showrunner' is not an official job title, but is often used when referring to 21st-century **Doctor Who** for the Executive Producer with script responsibility. At the time of writing **Doctor Who** has had only two showrunners in this sense, Russell T Davies and Steven Moffat.

[5] *Into the Dalek* (with Phil Ford), *Listen* (solo), *Time Heist* (with Stephen Thompson) and *The Caretaker* (with Gareth Roberts) (all

14

Deep Breath had taken pains not to appear anticlimactic following the previous year's festivities, opening with a dinosaur on the rampage in Victorian London and going on to employ the retro-futurist 'steampunk' aesthetic which had been the visual hallmark of some of **Doctor Who**'s most successful episodes[6], mixed with a splash of body horror. It continued in a small way the 'multiple Doctors' motif of every story since *The Name of the Doctor* (2013), with a farewell cameo from the 11th Doctor to seal the tentatively re-established trust between his successor and Clara, the companion he bequeathed him. The episode established further continuity touchpoints with Moffat's scripts for each of Capaldi's precursors since 2005: it revisited the 11th Doctor's mismatched allies Jenny, Strax and Madame Vastra, introduced in *A Good Man Goes to War* (2011) and last seen in *The Name of the Doctor*; it featured monsters with the same origin story as those in the 10th Doctor story *The Girl in the Fireplace* (2006); and it climaxed with the Doctor's antagonist impaled on the spire of Big Ben, whose tower had also featured significantly in Moffat's first script for the

---

2014). He also wrote the 2014 Christmas episode, *Last Christmas*, which followed seven weeks after *Death in Heaven*.

[6] Most recently *The Crimson Horror* (2013), but: 'Steampunk was anticipated several times in the UK television series **Doctor Who**, notably in *The Talons of Weng Chiang* (1977)' (Nicholls, Peter, and David Langford, 'Steampunk'). The article rather unadventurously defines 'steampunk' as 'the modern subgenre whose SF events take place against a 19th-century background': more detailed definitions are available.

revived series, the ninth Doctor story *The Empty Child / The Doctor Dances* (2005)[7].

Finally, *Deep Breath* closed with an introductory cameo for Michelle Gomez as Missy, a black-clad psychopomp inducting said deceased villain into the realm of the dead[8]. Viewers familiar with Moffat's plotting techniques in previous seasons would have been aware that this character would likely become crucial in the season finale, and the theory that she was the latest incarnation of the Doctor's schoolfriend and archenemy the Master was available to viewers from shortly after the episode aired[9]. The character reappeared for one-line or silent cameos in later episodes of the season: *Into the Dalek* and *The Caretaker* reinforced her psychopompic role, but *Flatline* and *In the Forest of the Night* suggested that she was keeping more general tabs on the Doctor's life, with a special interest in Clara (all episodes, 2014).

Into the Dalek, the season's second episode, also introduced Danny Pink, the maths teacher and ex-army sergeant who would become Clara's boyfriend and the season's other regular character (though never a passenger in the TARDIS[10]). With the exception of *Robot of*

---

[7] And in the 11th Doctor's own opening story, *The Eleventh Hour* (2010), which opens rather than ending with a scene of airborne peril over the spire.

[8] A psychopomp is a 'conductor of souls to the place of the dead' (*Oxford English Dictionary*), more usually in mythology or religion.

[9] See for instance Holmes, Jonathan, 'Doctor Who: Who Is Missy?'.

[10] Danny's dubious 'companion' status is thus most directly comparable with that of Liz Shaw, the third Doctor's assistant during the first year of his exile on Earth; although in terms of their

Sherwood, Danny appeared in every subsequent episode of 2014, his background and relationships with Clara and the Doctor being developed particularly in *Listen*, *The Caretaker* and *In the Forest of the Night*. By the time of *Dark Water / Death in Heaven*, the Doctor, Clara and Danny had all been given clear character arcs, which intersected in the finale with Missy's more obscure concerns.

The season, then, had carefully set up the conditions for a two-part finale, the programme's first since 2010. For the most part *Dark Water / Death in Heaven* would resolve these multiple plot threads with aplomb, in a story which also provided exemplary televisual spectacle. Like *Deep Breath*, the final two-parter reunited the 12th Doctor with some of his predecessor's allies: in this case Kate Stewart, the head of UNIT first seen in *The Power of Three* (2012)[11] and her assistant Osgood, introduced in *The Day of the Doctor*

---

influence on Clara at least, he might be better considered the Doctor's antagonist.

[11] The exact truth is more complex than this: Kate is rare example of a TV character who originated, in name at least, in **Doctor Who** spinoff media. Specifically, a 'Kate Lethbridge-Stewart', the Brigadier's daughter, played by Beverley Cressman rather than Jemma Redgrave, appears in the video dramas *Downtime* (Reeltime Pictures, 1995) and *Dæmos Rising* (Reeltime Pictures, 2004), and is occasionally mentioned (usually as a child in the 70s) in Virgin Publishing's **Doctor Who Missing Adventures** and **New Adventures** novels. *The Power of Three* effectively reimagines Kate, keeping little but two-thirds of her name, her family relationship with the Brigadier and her hair colour. *Downtime*'s scriptwriter Marc Platt has not been credited for the character's TV appearances.

(2013). It owed as much to the model for season finales created by Moffat's predecessor as showrunner, Russell T Davies, as to his own previous work in this area; in particular in placing contemporary Earth (and especially London) in jeopardy from an combination of villains familiar from 20th-century **Doctor Who**. Indeed, the 12th Doctor's 2014 character arc was indebted in some of its specifics to that of the ninth Doctor in the 2005 season.

However, Moffat goes beyond the immediate need to consolidate the success of Capaldi's first season with a robust, if traditional, two-part finale. The character of the Master has been much reinvented during the programme's history, but Missy, and her ambivalent relationship with the Doctor, represents a reimagining which is arguably more radical than in any prior reintroduction of a recurring villain. Like the 2013 anniversary material, the story reached beyond 21st-century continuity into the series' deep past, to homage an iconic scene from a **Doctor Who** story of decades before, and to resurrect an even more iconic character who appeared in that story, in an even more surprising form. It also functioned as a seasonal 'special', akin to the Christmas specials but attuned to the festivals of Halloween and Remembrance Day – and in the process addressed, with some seriousness, themes of grief and remembrance, war, and survival after death. Where *Deep Breath* borrowed from steampunk, *Dark Water / Death in Heaven* may also be Steven Moffat's closest approach to the near-future SF subgenre of cyberpunk[12].

---

[12] For a discussion of cyberpunk, see Chapter 6.

18

In its complexity, its thematic depth and its skilful interlacing of emotional and science-fictional plotting, *Dark Water / Death in Heaven* was not only the most successful season finale Steven Moffat had yet produced, it was perhaps also the most successful since the first year of the series' revival, which introduced the concept of the 'season finale' to **Doctor Who** in the first place.

CHAPTER 1. 'EVERYONE IN LONDON JUST CLAPPED': THE SEASON FINALE

As the culmination of the 34th full season of **Doctor Who**, *Dark Water / Death in Heaven* is profoundly a work of series drama, located firmly within a continuing narrative which has – as the audience was vividly reminded during the previous year – more than 50 years of history behind it.

This context is visible on multiple chronological scales. At the one extreme, the two-parter follows on closely from *In the Forest of the Night*, tying off the plot threads that have been braided throughout the 2014 episodes; it also ends the season (for the first time since *Last of the Time Lords* (2007)) with a narrative sting which introduces an element of the Christmas special. At the other extreme, it assembles elements – the Cybermen, UNIT, the villain previously known as the Master – first created for **Doctor Who** in the 1960s and 1970s, and reprises specific elements of an earlier encounter between the first and second of these, *The Invasion* (1968). Between these extremes of scale, medium-length strands of continuity stretch back to Clara's induction as a full-time companion in *The Bells of Saint John* (2013), the Master's last overt appearance *in The End of Time* (2009-10), and the Time War that occupies the gap in the fictive chronology between *Doctor Who* (1996) and *Rose* (2005). The story features explicit flashbacks to five previous stories, and of its 20 credited cast, more than half (to whom by far the majority of screen-time is devoted) play the same parts in other **Doctor Who** episodes[13].

At the same time, and with equal importance, *Dark Water / Death in Heaven* needs to function in the moment, as a self-sufficient hour and 45 minutes of television – as a spectacle, in fact, able to capture and retain the attention of intermittent, casual or entirely new viewers who may care surprisingly little that Ingrid Oliver's character shares her surname with a UNIT sergeant in the Jon Pertwee story *The Dæmons* (1971). While this is of course true of every contemporary **Doctor Who** story, the season finales, like the Christmas specials, come with higher expectations. The fact that these expectations are largely based on precedent since 2005 makes them no less important.

Between these two sets of demands there is an inevitable tension. While some viewers might feel dubious about the level of continuity involved in this story, its marriage of deep history with immediate spectacle is as productive here as in the best season finales of the 21st century.

---

[13] Samuel Anderson, Jenna Coleman, Sheila Reid, Peter Capaldi, Chris Addison, Michelle Gomez, Ingrid Oliver and Jemma Redgrave make return appearances. Nigel Betts and Nick Briggs speak but are not seen. Bradley Ford (as Fleming, Danny's cadet at Coal Hill School who appeared in *Into the Dalek*) is credited but neither appears nor speaks; one assumes that the school's memorial assembly for Danny was filmed, but only the voiceover of Armitage's address was used. Nick Frost has not appeared previously, but will be the major guest star of *Last Christmas*. Only eight other actors receive credits, and only three of their characters even have names.

Before this century, with one arguable exception, there were no 'finales' in the currently-recognised sense. Like its close relative the Christmas special, the **Doctor Who** 'season finale' is essentially an innovation of Russell T Davies's tenure as showrunner (2005-10). In the 20th century there were certainly 'event' stories which ended one phase of the narrative and ushered in a new one; generally these are those where the actor playing the Doctor changes or a long-running character is written out. However, the former are no more likely, and the latter actually less likely, to come at the end of a season than during one[14].

The nearest approach in 20th-century **Doctor Who** to the model of the modern season finale comes at the end of *The War Games* (1969). Consisting of 10 25-minute episodes, this serial forms a narrative unit of comparable length to the halves of the split seasons of 2011 and 2012-13. Its concluding episodes focus on the character of Patrick Troughton's Doctor to an unusual degree,

---

[14] Of the 25 (at least) acknowledged 20th-century companions, the only ones to depart at the end of a season are Jamie and Zoe (*The War Games*, 1969), Jo (*The Green Death*, 1973), Leela (*The Invasion of Time*, 1978 – she takes one model of K-9 with her, but another replaces him) and Mel (*Dragonfire*, 1987). Liz (*Inferno*, 1970), Mike Yates (*Planet of the Spiders*, 1974 – although his status as a companion is dubious) and Ace (*Survival*, 1989) are last seen at the end of a season, but have no 'departure story' as such. Of the 20th-century 'regeneration' stories (to use the terminology only coined in 1974), *The War Games*, *Planet of the Spiders* and *Logopolis* (1981) come at the end of their respective seasons; *The Tenth Planet* (1966), *The Caves of Androzani* (1984) and *Time and the Rani* (1987) do not. (*Doctor Who* (1996) stands outside the season structure.)

22

revealing new information about him and culminating in an unprecedented return to his home planet; they end with the departure of two long-term companions **and** a change of lead actor, from Troughton to Pertwee; they function as a visual spectacle, using time-travel as a mechanism to throw together characters from multiple historical periods with futuristic aliens in a manner not unreminiscent of 2011's season finale, *The Wedding of River Song* (2011); and – as the final episodes to be broadcast in black-and-white, and the ones to establish the third Doctor's confinement to Earthbound adventures – they bring with them more than the usual sense of closure.

The War Games is an anomaly, however – in terms of its unique positioning, its length, and its scope to reveal details that had so far been kept from the viewer – and would not recur during the 20th century. In the 1970s and 80s, such connected sequences of stories as there are – for instance the tetralogy bookended by the two 'Nerva Beacon' stories[15], or the two trilogies reformatting the series for the Peter Davison era[16] – occur ad hoc within, or occasionally across, seasons. Only in *The Armageddon Factor* (1979), 'The Ultimate Foe' (*The Trial of a Time Lord* episodes 13–14, 1986) and just possibly *Time-Flight* (1982) do identifiable 'story

---

[15] *The Ark in Space, The Sontaran Experiment, Genesis of the Daleks* and *Revenge of the Cybermen* (all 1975).
[16] *Full Circle, State of Decay* and *Warriors' Gate* (all 1981), which write out Romana and K-9 and introduce the character of Adric; and *The Keeper of Traken* and *Logopolis* (both 1981) and *Castrovalva* (1982), which introduce Nyssa and Tegan, regenerate the Doctor and re-establish the Master as a regular villain.

arcs' end with a season[17], and never with the sense of occasion that a 21st-century season finale brings. Even the last regular story of the 20th century, *Survival* (1989), acknowledges its placement only in its final seconds, as Sylvester McCoy delivers in a hastily-added voiceover the valedictory speech which would stand for 16 years as the show's interim epitaph.

This was partly due to the nature of series television during **Doctor Who**'s original run: while the series was exceptional in being constructed out of multi-episode serials, most of these serials were designed, like the individual episodes of more conventional dramas, for standalone accessibility by the casual viewer, and to facilitate out-of-context repeats – as happened, for instance, with *The Evil of the Daleks* (1967) in 1968, or with the various stories chosen for the **Five Faces of Doctor Who** anthology season in 1981.

Even more rarely do these stories attempt anything more visually impressive or narratively memorable than is routine for their period: *The War Games* again excepted, there is no sense that these are occasions for spectacular 'event' television[18]. Arguable exceptions might include the fourth Doctor's flashbacks to companions and enemies saying his name before his demise[19], the

---

[17] Respectively the search for the Key to Time, the Doctor's second trial by the Time Lords, and the very loose 'Tegan would like to get back to Heathrow Airport' arc.

[18] 20th-century **Doctor Who** is rarely 'spectacular' in the manner of the 21st-century series, largely because of and the limitations of contemporary special-effects technologies and its strictly controlled budget for them.

[19] *Logopolis* episode 4.

fifth Doctor's hallucinatory cameos from his past companions at the moment of his[20], or even the montage of contemporary London scenes which signals Ian and Barbara's return home[21], but all of these are minor and fleeting elements of their respective stories, and tangential rather than crucial to the narrative. The idea of structuring a script primarily around such a sequence (as *The End of Time* episode 2 is structured) was decades away.

As a pilot that did not result in a series, *Doctor Who* (1996) did not have to address the question of how to structure its seasons. The 'Leekley Bible' of 1994 – a set of plans for a rebooted series of **Doctor Who** which strongly influenced the pilot that was later made – gives the Doctor an ongoing motivation in the quest for his vanished father Ulysses, but most of its suggestions for individual episodes are standalone re-imaginings of 1963-89 stories[22].

In 2005, the revived series faced a radically different set of audience expectations, shaped by experience of such US SF and fantasy series as **Babylon 5** (1993-1998), **The X-Files** (1993-2002, 2016-) and **Buffy the Vampire Slayer** (1997-2003). Changing production and viewing technologies had trained viewers, particularly the devoted fanbases attracted by genre television, to revisit and re-examine prior episodes in ways which the **Doctor Who** of the past had not generally been constructed to support. Earlier genre dramas had been notorious for their 'reset button' plotting which – aside from the occasional need to write out cast

---

[20] *The Caves of Androzani* episode 4.
[21] 'The Planet of Decision' (*The Chase* episode 6, 1965).
[22] Segal, Philip, with Gary Russell, *Doctor Who: Regeneration*, pp43-58.

members and introduce their replacements – returned the regular characters and their setup to the status quo at the end of the episode, no matter how life-changing their experiences might have been expected to be. By the end of the 1990s, such drama was generally expected to tell stories that progressed from one episode and one season to the next, developing its characters and placing them in constantly changing situations[23].

As Jon Arnold discusses in *The Black Archive #1: Rose*, Russell T Davies's 2005 revival of **Doctor Who** was concerned to appear vibrant and contemporary to its viewers, rather than a retread of a programme which had slipped into oblivion a decade and a half before. Where *Doctor Who* (1996) had drawn heavily on **The X-Files**[24], Davies's **Doctor Who** took some of its cues from the enormously popular **Buffy**, one of whose defining features was the season-long arc plot leading to confrontations with a 'Big Bad' villain particular to that season – although the most vital of these

---

[23] The contrast is perhaps most evident in the development of the **Star Trek** franchise: **The Next Generation** (1987-94) is largely content to follow the former model, while **Deep Space Nine** (1993-99) clearly aspires to the latter, despite the overlap in production chronology.

[24] The influence is most strongly visible in the central dynamic of an eccentric male protagonist of whose wild claims his female partner is sceptical; in making the latter a medical doctor with a scientific interest in extraterrestrial matters; and most blatantly in the sequence where her vaguely sinister boss destroys all the evidence of her patient's true nature with a cigarette lighter. Part of this commonality may be due to the fact that both are Fox co-productions, filmed in Vancouver (and even sharing certain locations).

developing cruxes generally related not to the machinations of the villains, but to the regular characters and their relationships. This model places a weight of expectation on the season finale as the point where such events come to a head, and accordingly final episodes under Davies were radically changed; but so were the overall shapes of seasons, whose episodes became more interconnected and more ordered.

Davies's first year as showrunner rises to this challenge with near-platonic perfection, establishing a close symmetry across the season[25]. Arc plotting is tight, seeding multiple elements across the episodes which will become crucial at the season's emotional climax. Rose's rejection of the mundane certainties of her old life and her willingness to break the rules for those she loves becomes central in the finale, while the Doctor – portrayed as experiencing survivor guilt and paralysing indecision following the Time War – faces a question of his own moral identity. A leitmotif emerges, as the words 'Bad Wolf' echo in various marginal contexts throughout Earth's history.

---

[25] If *Rose* and *The End of the World* are considered as a two-parter introducing Rose to the Doctor, a symmetrical, almost crystalline structure of similarities emerges across the 13 stories. For instance, both *Aliens of London / World War Three* (episodes 4 to 5) and *The Empty Child / The Doctor Dances* (episodes 9 to 10) feature appearance-changing alien technologies, bombs, Big Ben, the Albion Hospital, confidence tricks involving spaceships, and allusions relating the Doctor to a fairytale wolf (his chasing the pig and Nancy pointing out what big ears he has). *The Long Game* (episode 7) thus acts as the season's fulcrum, and indeed its events turn out in *Bad Wolf* to have been pivotal. (All episodes 2005.)

In *The Parting of the Ways* (2005) these elements intersect elegantly, as the Doctor's and Rose's attempts to protect one another ultimately trigger the end of his ninth (acknowledged) incarnation. The question of the Doctor's morality is made explicit by the Dalek Emperor ('What are you, coward or killer?'), and he resolves it by refusing to repeat his act of genocide: 'Coward. Any day.'[26]

No season since has achieved quite the same tooled precision as the Christopher Eccleston Doctor's story arc. Davies's seasons in particular demonstrate diminishing returns in terms of plotting, until by 2008 the 'arc story' for the season consists of a few shapeless references to disappearing planets, vanishing bees and the coming end of Donna's travels with the Doctor, with some enigmatic appearances by Billie Piper as Rose. What Davies puts in its place is visual spectacle.

Bad Wolf / The Parting of the Ways is certainly not deficient in this area – serving up visual pastiches of various contemporary game shows, a Dalek battlefleet and the impressive Emperor Dalek design – but its main storyline is a claustrophobic base-under-siege plot with excursions to 20th-century London and a Dalek spaceship, and its Dalek assault on 2,001st-century Earth takes place wholly off-screen. All the season finales of David Tennant's tenure as the Doctor follow a formula drawing on elements from other 2005 stories (specifically *Rose* and *Aliens of London / World War Three*), and designed to give such episodes a greater visual and dramatic impact.

---

[26] *The Parting of the Ways.*

Accordingly, from *Army of Ghosts / Doomsday* (2006) to *The End of Time*, it is always **contemporary** Earth that is in peril[27]. This peril consists of large armies of aliens threatening (or sometimes replacing) the entire planetary population; and is shown directly – locally through its effect on the companion's family and on prominent London landmarks, and globally by news clips and brief cutaways to events outside Britain. As in *Bad Wolf / The Parting of the Ways*, the finales bring back high-profile enemies from the series' past, often in combination. Guest characters from recent years also return, sometimes in startling numbers, while guest stars ranging in cultural significance from Richard Dawkins to Sharon Osbourne appear as themselves[28].

Finally, these finales escalate, each bidding to outdo its predecessor, until by *The End of Time* the entire universe, not merely the Earth, is being threatened not with conquest but with existential annihilation. This, more than anything else, is what makes this model unsustainable in the longer term. Regardless of its success during Davies's tenure as showrunner, it was inevitable that when Steven Moffat took over he would have to try something different.

Accordingly, Moffat's season finales dial back to some extent on the grandiose melodrama, but reintroduce a greater degree of

---

[27] For the 00s stories' standard value of 'contemporary', which is to say a year or so in the future.
[28] In *Journey's End* (2008) and *The Sound of Drums* (2007) respectively. Admittedly this does not happen in *The End of Time*, where President Obama is played by an actor. Some casting coups are beyond even BBC Cardiff's reach.

interconnection within and between seasons. While a modified pattern emerges in his season finales between 2010 and 2013, more noticeable is their variety, an avoidance of the formula of the Davies years.

During 11th Doctor Matt Smith's season finales, the peril faced remains universal in scope, but the critical action plays out on a smaller scale and the stakes for the Doctor are more personal, often involving his anticipated death[29]. The significance of the monsters is played down – the 2010 two-parter's first episode, *The Pandorica Opens*, features a crowd-pleasing coalition of familiar aliens, but they do little except emphasise the odds stacked against the Doctor, and the enemy forces in the second part, *The Big Bang*, consist of a solitary fossil Dalek. The returning characters continue to varying extents, but the real-world guest faces are phased out. In short, the spectacle is toned down, and the stories rely on other incentives to draw in the audience.

More obviously, there is a structural move away from the Davies-era standard of the two-part finale, with *The Wedding of River Song* a standalone episode introduced by a brief coda to *Closing Time* (2011), and *The Name of the Doctor* best viewed as a single-part prelude to *The Day of the Doctor*. (Of the two 'mid-season finales,' *A Good Man Goes to War* was billed as the first half of a split two-

---

[29] In Davies's finales, we were more often led to believe that the companion's death is inevitable: see (most obviously) Rose's 'This is where I died' in *Army of Ghosts*.

parter[30] and *The Angels Take Manhattan* (2012) is a standalone episode.)

This is accompanied by the return to complex continuing plot threads. In this Moffat is more ambitious than Davies, but rarely as successful. To some extent it can be said that, that while the function of a season finale is in part to conclude the arc story of the preceding season, it is equally part of the function of a 21st-century season to set up an arc story that can be satisfactorily concluded in the finale, and in this Moffat's seasons have had mixed success.

Thus *The Pandorica Opens* / *The Big Bang* promisingly brings together the visual leitmotif of the crack in space with the troubled development of Amy's relationship with Rory, the 'spoilers' provided by River Song in *The Time of Angels* / *Flesh and Stone*, and a complex chain of historical causality involving characters from *The Beast Below*, *Victory of the Daleks* and *Vincent and the Doctor* (all 2010), along with River herself (who first appeared in *Silence in the Library* / *Forest of the Dead* (2008)). Unfortunately, it leaves major elements dangling (the 'silence' which supposedly 'will fall' and the mysterious voice responsible for the averted destruction of the TARDIS) which will be ignored for some years and only resolved, not very satisfactorily, in Matt Smith's farewell story, *The Time of the Doctor*.

Indeed, *The Time of the Doctor* and the episodes which precede it see an almost comedic domino cascade of what could otherwise have been longer-term plot elements: *The Name of the Doctor* ends the story of the 11th Doctor's relationship with River and

---

[30] With *Let's Kill Hitler* (2011).

31

resolves the status of Clara as 'the Impossible Girl', but also predicts the Doctor's death at Trenzalore and unveils a mysterious past incarnation of the Doctor who has appeared in none of the previous rosters; *The Day of the Doctor* (with the help of 'The Night of the Doctor' (2013)) explains John Hurt's Doctor adequately while establishing that Gallifrey has not been destroyed but is hidden away in another universe; and *The Time of the Doctor* not only resolves the Trenzalore prophecy, along with the dangling plot elements from 2010, but introduces **and then immediately solves** the hitherto-unmentioned problem that the Doctor has reached the end of his regeneration cycle. Watching Smith's final episode particularly, a sense that Moffat had at least another season's worth of material planned for the 11th Doctor and is giving us the edited highlights, to clear the decks before the 12th incarnation's arrival, becomes almost inescapable.

The more ambitious a set of plot threads is, then, the harder a showrunner will have to work to resolve them successfully, but the more satisfying the result. Probably few viewers were very impressed by the way *The Stolen Earth / Journey's End* (2008) explained about the bees, but equally few would have placed much weight on the question, or finished the season complaining of dangling plot strands. Moffat's declaration that the 2012-13 season would consist of 'blockbuster of the week' episodes whose concept could fit into a movie poster suggests an awareness that this aspect of the series had not been working as well as it could have [31].

---

[31] Martin, Dan, 'Doctor Who: Asylum of the Daleks – spoiler-free review'.

32

At the time of broadcast, it seemed that *Dark Water / Death in Heaven* might represent a permanent return to Davies's model of season closure. However, as the concluding episodes of the 2015 series reject the formula once more – the penultimate *Heaven Sent* being particularly experimental – this idea can be dismissed[32]. It seems that the diversity of Moffat's finales – an approach which can accommodate a range of formats, scenarios, settings and storytelling techniques to produce *Heaven Sent / Hell Bent* (2015) or *The Name of the Doctor* – can also accommodate a Tennant-style two-parter featuring a team-up of old enemies, set on contemporary Earth and told as a (mostly) linear narrative.

Clearly, though, *Dark Water / Death in Heaven* does directly borrow some elements of Davies's pattern. As in the Tennant finales, contemporary Earth is in peril, as one of the 20th century series' most prominent villains deploys an army of one of its most familiar monster species over the London skyline and globally ('New York, Paris, Rome, Marrakesh, Brisbane... Glasgow' according

---

[32] *Face the Raven, Heaven Sent* and *Hell Bent* (all 2015). While at the time of writing Wikipedia persists in referring to these as a 'three-part finale' – and certainly their events lead directly into one another – the change in writer and director between *Face the Raven* and *Heaven Sent*, not to mention the clue in the titles, suggests a much stronger connection between the latter two stories. (Alternatively, since *Heaven Sent* is isolated in setting from the other two stories and features no characters other than the Doctor, their individual peculiarities mean they could validly be considered a series of three linked single-part stories.) A future **Black Archive** title is planned which will address *Face the Raven* as a story in its own right.

33

to Missy, as she flicks past images on her phone[33]). Like the Toclafane in *The Sound of Drums / Last of the Time Lords* (2007) and the 'Master Race' in *The End of Time*, these Cybermen are not merely menacing humanity but are in the process of replacing it. For Clara the threat is immediate and personal, directly affecting a recurring character connected to her. As in many Davies stories (and a couple of earlier Moffat ones), a well-known London landmark plays a prominent part[34].

At the same time, the concerns of the Smith finales are still visible. The monsters' impact on Clara is through a boyfriend, not a blood relative as was generally the case for Tennant's companions – and unlike those family members he fails to survive the experience. (In a Davies finale Clara's Gran, who appears in *Dark Water* but is nowhere to be seen in *Death in Heaven*, would very likely have been visiting a graveyard at the time of the Cybermen's rising.) While the threat is global, the climax of the episodes comes in a lengthy scene involving only four people[35]. Although the monsters

---

[33] *Death in Heaven*.

[34] Davies's use of London landmarks is not confined to his season endings, but is a feature of most of his contemporary Earth stories. The stories from 2005-10 make prominent use of the London Eye, Big Ben, 10 Downing Street, the Tower of London, the Gherkin, Battersea Power Station, Canary Wharf Tower, the Thames Flood Barrier and Buckingham Palace. Moffat makes less use of such imagery, but his scripts incorporate the Shard (*The Bells of Saint John*), the Tower of London again (*The Day of the Doctor*) and Big Ben again (*The Eleventh Hour*, *Deep Breath*).

[35] Although it fits the story's themes, and the presence of multiple Cybermen is helpful for illustrative purposes, within the fiction there is no clear reason for the characters to be in the graveyard.

take part in spectacular sequences, with the exception of Danny and the Brigadier they have no independent agency and say little[36], mostly stumbling around disorientated while the Doctor's psychodrama plays itself out. Although the 12th Doctor is not anticipating death on this occasion (that will come the next year in *The Magician's Apprentice* (2015)), the moral temptation Missy brings is a threat to his survival as the Doctor we know.

Most obviously, multiple plot elements from earlier episodes of 2014 are teased out, displayed and – for the most part – tied off neatly. *Dark Water / Death in Heaven* manages the balance between complex plotting and satisfying resolution considerably more effectively than Moffat's previous finales. With two exceptions – the quest for Gallifrey (which is developed, not resolved, in these episodes), and the lingering question of who gave Clara the Doctor's phone number in *The Bells of Saint John* –

Missy follows the Doctor there; the Doctor is seeking Clara; and Clara was taken there by Danny – an odd thing for him to do when he has just rescued her from other Cybermen. A similar consideration applies to the Brigadier (who we might suppose is following the Doctor or Missy) and Kate. As a Cyberman in the background of the scene can be heard repeating 'Locate hive', we can only assume that Danny has been impelled by his conditioning to seek the company of other Cybermen.

[36] The Brigadier Cyberman does not speak onscreen, but for Kate to be aware that it is her father it has presumably addressed her offscreen.

the pressing issues facing the finale are only those set up within the preceding season, and these it mostly addresses skilfully[37].

The story does not neglect its televisual pyrotechnics, however. Although striking and novel imagery is, and should be, a regular feature of **Doctor Who**, and the 50th anniversary festivities involved some spectacular examples, the specific kind of showmanship involved in a Tennant finale – with hordes of ray-gun-wielding aliens disrupting the comforting rhythm of contemporary life, massive flying objects and the Doctor placed in extravagant peril – has been largely absent in Moffat's finales. *Dark Water / Death in Heaven* provides both kinds of visuals, supplying the hollow-Earth cityscape of the Nethersphere, the dead rising from their graves in metal armour and a visit from Father Christmas; but also the dome of St Paul's Cathedral opening up to emit a swarm of flying Cybermen, a jet plane being dismantled in flight, and the Doctor rendezvousing with the TARDIS during the course of an otherwise fatal plummet.

Following the success of 2013's celebration of **Doctor Who**'s past – which had seen Jenna Coleman and Richard E Grant digitally nserted into scenes from *Arc of Infinity* (1983), *The Five Doctors* (1983) and *Dragonfire* (1987)[38], extensive reconstructions of 1960s studio filming[39], and various techniques used to recreate past Doctors[40] – *Dark Water / Death in Heaven* is bolder than pre-2013

---

[37] For a detailed treatment of these, see Chapter 2.
[38] *The Name of the Doctor.*
[39] *An Adventure in Space and Time.*
[40] Including digitally compositing them into new scenes (*The Name of the Doctor*), dressing extras in familiar costumes and wigs (*The*

season finales in pitching some of its spectacles specifically at the **Doctor Who** fan audience. (Davies in particular was cautious about this: he may have been happy in a routine weekly episode to revive a monster from an obscure 40-year-old story which only survives in audio form [41], but his finales used only the most universally recognisable elements of the series' 20th-century past – the Daleks, the Cybermen, the Master, Davros.)

Not all of the scenes which could have been are so pitched. Conceptually, the image of Cybermen returning to life in a mausoleum owes a clear debt to *The Tomb of the Cybermen* (1967), and could have been made to reflect it, but visually (and in terms of plot and themes, inasmuch as *The Tomb of the Cybermen* has either) *Dark Water* has little in common with that story.

Another 20th-century story which presents apparent similarities with *Dark Water / Death in Heaven* is the Jon Pertwee story *The Dæmons*. On the face of it, these parallels might seem striking. Both stories evoke major festivals of the pagan year, Beltane and Samhain [42]. Both draw on horror-movie imagery while ostensibly explaining away a major element of Christian doctrine (the Devil in *The Dæmons*, Heaven in *Dark Water*). Peter Capaldi's 2014

Name of the Doctor), combining archive footage with voice work by impersonators (*The Day of the Doctor*) and simply filming new scenes with the surviving actors ('The Night of the Doctor', *The Day of the Doctor*).

[41] The Macra, first seen in *The Macra Terror* (1967) and revived in *Gridlock* (2007).

[42] See Chapter 3 for a discussion of this in *Dark Water / Death in Heaven*.

costume is reminiscent of Pertwee's, and the semi-regular cast in *Dark Water / Death in Heaven* include female equivalents (Missy, Kate [Lethbridge-]Stewart and Osgood) of several characters from the Pertwee era – one of whose originals, Sergeant Osgood, appears only in *The Dæmons*. In both stories, the Master sets up shop in a church and attempts to weaponise an alien species. Both stories culminate with a villain defeated by the willingness of a regular character (Jo Grant and Danny Pink respectively) to sacrifice themselves to save another.

On further examination, however, the analogy is a superficial one. The use of horror imagery is far from rare in **Doctor Who**, and the seasonal association of *Dark Water / Death in Heaven* – implied, not explicit as is *The Dæmons*'s with Beltane – is with the popular Halloween, not its neo-pagan equivalent. The association of Capaldi's Doctor with Pertwee's extends to assigning him a new Master and a revamped UNIT as semi-regular characters[43], and is – for the most part – not a specific reference to *The Dæmons*: Missy and Kate are fixtures of Capaldi's tenure only slightly less than the Master and the Brigadier are of the Pertwee era. Using a church as a location in a story which addresses Christian doctrine is not especially surprising; and in the case of *Dark Water / Death in Heaven* owes more to the decision to recreate an iconic scene from a quite different early UNIT story. The Master has a long history of using other species to his own ends, from the Autons in *Terror of the Autons* (1971) to the Toclafane in *The Sound of Drums*[44]. Self-

---

[43] Both reappear in 2015, beginning with the first episode of the season, *The Magician's Apprentice*.
[44] See Chapter 4 for more on this.

sacrifice is a trope so common in **Doctor Who** as to be almost ubiquitous.

The differences are more significant. *The Dæmons'* thematic heart lies in the debate (such as it is, given that the deck is stacked hugely in the Doctor's favour) between the Doctor's scientific worldview and the magical thinking of the white witch Miss Hawthorne. *Dark Water / Death in Heaven* has little of this beyond the Doctor's dismissal of Dr Skarosa as 'an idiot': he is prepared to accept the afterlife as a hypothesis for the sake of helping Clara, and he turns out to be justified. The Delgado Master's earlier plan has little in common with the Gomez incarnation's here (specifically, it is to invoke a being with godlike powers and talk it into making him ruler of the Earth), and the way the plots unfold is dissimilar.

The only lingering affinity seems to involve the mirror-inversion of three characters' genders (which might optimistically be related to the opposition of Beltane and Samhain on the wheel of the year, as the beginnings of spring and autumn respectively), and in particular the recurrence of the name 'Osgood'. The Pertwee era in general is frequently described as sexist, but *The Dæmons* in particular characterises its women as irrational (in Jo Grant's case, sufficiently so to confuse the Devil to death) while placing the tools of rational thought in the hands of the paternalistic Doctor. In this respect, naming a competent female scientist after the Brigadier's technician might be seen as a rebuke to the 1970s story... but while Sergeant Osgood appears only in *The Dæmons*, his namesake has appeared previously in 2013 and will again in 2015 (despite her death here). While the name is clearly a reference to *The Dæmons*, it ties *The Day of the Doctor* and *The Zygon Invasion / The Zygon Inversion* (2015) to the Pertwee story exactly as much as it does

39

Dark Water / Death in Heaven. In the end, these apparent parallels boil down to little more than formula and coincidence.

By contrast, the homage to a second Troughton-era Cyberman story is quite deliberate[45]. The influence of *The Invasion* on *Dark Water / Death in Heaven* is apparent in a number of story elements. The severed Cyber-head which Kate presents to the Cybermen along with her credentials is of the design used in the earlier episodes, and her reference to 'one of your previous attempts' is a direct reference. Indeed, *The Invasion* was the only time in the 20th century that Cybermen were seen trying to invade contemporary Earth[46]. It introduced UNIT and represents the only previous conflict between them and the Cybermen[47]. In both stories the Cybermen ally themselves with a humanoid villain, whose corporate front allows them to infiltrate contemporary Earth society. Both corporations have automated reception systems: International Electromatics's took the form of a 60s-style computer bank made out of tape reel and flashing lights, whereas

---

[45] **Doctor Who Extra** confirms this, if anyone felt it was in need of confirmation.

[46] Admittedly this relies on distinguishing between the near-future setting of *The Invasion* (set in a recognisable late-60s London with some additional technology) and the more dislocated futures of the stories set in Arctic bases, Moon colonies and orbiting space stations (even though the earliest of these, *The Tenth Planet*, is set only 20 years ahead in 1986). The small-scale incursions seen in *Attack of the Cybermen* (1985) and *Silver Nemesis* (1988) were not invasions.

[47] Colonel Lethbridge-Stewart, who as the Brigadier heads UNIT, was introduced previously in *The Web of Fear* (1968).

3W's is a holographic animation (supplemented by Missy pretending to be a robot). In both stories, the Doctor is kidnapped by UNIT and bundled aboard a plane – the only times to date the organisation had been seen using an aircraft as a mobile headquarters[48]. Both address concerns about human obsolescence and replacement, although this is an implicit theme of many Cyberman stories.

Most obviously, the final moments of *Dark Water* recreate an iconic scene from *The Invasion* episode 6 – directed by the highly-respected Douglas Camfield – in which Cybermen tramp down St Peter's Steps in Sermon Lane, London EC4, with the dome of St Paul's visible above their heads.

(Again this could be seen as following Davies's lead, although from his relaunch of **Doctor Who** rather than any of his finales. Prior to *Dark Water / Death in Heaven*, the closest recreation of a 20th-century **Doctor Who** scene in the 21st century came in *Rose*, where the scene of shop-window dummies coming to murderous life mimics, without directly replicating, an equally memorable scene from *Spearhead from Space* episode four.)

In *The Invasion* this shot began a montage of similar footage of Cybermen at loose in London which led into the episode's cliffhanger, but in the hands of *Dark Water / Death in Heaven*'s director Rachel Talalay it becomes the centrepiece of the cliffhanger: a dramatic climax following the Doctor's reaction to

---

[48] Despite being destroyed here, Bird One (presumably a different plane) is seen again in *The Zygon Invasion / The Zygon Inversion*, where it is also destroyed.

41

Missy's revelation of her identity and preceding a final sting shot of Danny in the Nethersphere, considering his options before the end credits.

Talalay's recreation is instantly evocative, but not slavishly literal. The grammar of TV has changed in 46 years, and in retrospect Camfield's shot appears languid, 15 seconds of footage of the Cybermen slowly coming into view at the top of the steps and beginning to descend. Talalay's version is pacier and more dynamic: a 10-second, three-shot sequence narrowing in on Cybermen who are descending throughout, leading into a lingering close-up of a Cyberman's eye which cuts to Danny[49]. To the long-term, dedicated or fan viewer, this may be the most effective scene in the two-parter, but even for the casual audience (who could be forgiven for not realising that it was a recreation at all) the composition remains a striking one, and creates an impact similar to that of the original. Although the homage is more direct, this is precisely the impression of the alien invading the mundane that the Tennant-era finales worked to evoke[50].

---

[49] The implied connection is thematic rather than physical: Danny is in the Nethersphere, which is located inside the Matrix data-slice, not in the Cybermen's heads. Danny is, however, considering a course of action which will turn him into a Cyberman, like whichever formerly-human consciousness is currently inhabiting the Cyberman on the steps.

[50] There is a famous quote from Jon Pertwee referring to 'a Yeti on the loo in Tooting Bec' which it is traditional to trot out at this point (*Myth Makers: Jon Pertwee*).

CHAPTER 2. 'I'VE BEEN UP AND DOWN YOUR TIMELINE': GATHERING THE THREADS

Since his regeneration, *Death in Heaven*'s 12th Doctor has, like his ninth incarnation, been plagued by questions about his moral identity. Where the question facing Eccleston's Doctor was whether he was 'a coward' or 'a killer', the equivalent for Peter Capaldi's is 'Am I a good man?'[51].

The question has, in fact, already been dismissed by Clara at the beginning of the episode where Capaldi's Doctor (or his eyebrows) first appears, in a quote from the Roman philosopher and emperor Marcus Aurelius: 'Waste no more time arguing about what a good man should be. Be one.'[52] In the same sequence of special episodes we learned that the eighth Doctor suffered little from such self-doubt prior to his involvement in the Time War[53] – although by his

---

[51] *Into the Dalek.*
[52] *The Day of the Doctor.* The self-indulgent futility of the question is underscored in 2015's *The Witch's Familiar*, when Davros of all people asks the Doctor, 'Was I right? [...] Am I a good man?'
[53] 'The Night of the Doctor':
> OHILA
> Because you are the good man, as you call yourself?
> DOCTOR
> I call myself the Doctor.
> OHILA
> It's the same thing in your mind.
> DOCTOR
> I'd like to think so.
NB: Where script books are unavailable, all dialogue from episodes (even when presented in script format) is transcribed from the broadcast episode.

11th incarnation, he had apparently changed his mind on the point[54].

For the 12th Doctor as for the ninth, the question is provoked by a solitary captive Dalek, afflicted in the absence of Dalek society by its own loss of moral certainty. Unsettled by his first encounter with the creature in *Into the Dalek*, the Doctor asks Clara, 'Be my pal and tell me – am I a good man?' Whereas the Dalek in *Dalek* (2005) told the Doctor 'You would make a good Dalek', 'Rusty'[55] goes further: 'I am not a good Dalek. You are a good Dalek.' The self-doubt this question reveals beneath this incarnation's arrogant and abrasive exterior is exacerbated by his encounter with Robin Hood, which extends the spectrum of (rejected) moral possibilities from 'Dalek' to 'hero'[56]. Although Clara is ambivalent when the Doctor first poses the question to her, she later agrees with Maisie in *Mummy on the Orient Express* (2014) that the Doctor is 'a good man', and Saibra in *Time Heist* (2014) comes independently to this conclusion. (On both occasions however, the judgement is undercut: the Doctor is about to use Maisie as bait for the titular Mummy, while the manipulative Architect who he has impressed Saibra by refusing to kill turns out to be himself.)

---

[54] *A Good Man Goes to War*: 'Good men don't need rules. Today is not the day to find out why I have so many.'

[55] Given the episode's debt to its 2005 predecessor, it is hard not to see the naming of the captive Dalek as a tribute to Russell T Davies, occasionally known to fans as 'Rusty', although *Dalek* was in fact written by Robert Shearman.

[56] *Robot of Sherwood*.

Further doubt is cast on the Doctor's moral status by Danny, who sees him as 'an officer', responsible for the deaths of ordinary soldiers like Danny himself[57]. The Doctor's attitude to the armed forces has long been one of impatience: the limitations of 'the military mind' (a favourite phrase[58]), and the tendency of soldiers to resort to violent solutions, are sources of frustration in a great many 20th-century stories, especially those where he collaborates with UNIT. Capaldi's incarnation, however, has been more than characteristically dismissive of soldiers. His antagonism is especially visible in *Into the Dalek*, where he repeatedly makes clear his dislike of Journey Blue's profession: the same episode sees Clara start dating Danny, for whom the Doctor reserves especial contempt. This arises before he learns of their relationship, apparently from Danny's being introduced to him as having 'five years' military experience'. It results in him regarding him as a 'PE teacher'[59], and refusing to believe he meets the intellectual requirements of his actual subject specialism, mathematics[60].

---

[57] *The Caretaker.*
[58] Used in, for instance, *The War Games* episode one, *The Silurians* episode two (1970) and *Battlefield* episode one (1989).
[59] Sports or 'Physical Education' (PE) teachers are stereotypically treated as stupid in British popular culture. Compare the **Red Dwarf** episode *Future Echoes* (1988): 'I am Holly, the ship's computer, with an IQ of 6,000 – the same IQ as 6,000 PE teachers.'
[60] *The Caretaker.* The fact that Danny is black has caused some viewers to read this as **racial** prejudice, particularly in view of the ninth and 10th Doctors' similar dismissal of the decidedly non-military Mickey as 'Mickey the idiot'. There is no particular reason to suppose that either Danny or Mickey were written as black

It can hardly be coincidental that the soldier to whom the Doctor has been shown as closest in the past – and with whom he was working in most of those 20th-century UNIT stories – also retired temporarily from military life to become, specifically, a maths teacher[61]. Although Brigadier Alistair Lethbridge-Stewart (played by Nicholas Courtney) last appeared in **Doctor Who** in *Battlefield* (1989)[62], he has been mentioned repeatedly in the 21st-century stories, most recently as the father of Kate Stewart, the head of UNIT in the Doctor's current timeframe. The long-term viewer – if not the Doctor – may well be reminded of his existence during *The Caretaker* itself by the forename of Danny and Clara's pupil Courtney Woods[63]. A more explicit reminder comes in *Death in Heaven*, when the Brigadier's portrait is seen aboard the Presidential plane, Boat One, and Kate reveals that his 'big ambition' was for the Doctor to salute him – a particularly military gesture of respect.

---

characters rather than cast with black actors, but the coincidence is a slightly uncomfortable one.

[61] *Mawdryn Undead* (1983).

[62] Although in fact the character made a rather dismal last appearance in the **Sarah Jane Adventures** story *Enemy of the Bane* (2008).

[63] Courtney first appears, briefly, in *Deep Breath* and again in *Into the Dalek*, and is a major character in *The Caretaker* and *Kill the Moon* (2014). That the choice of her name was deliberate may be implied by the fact that at an earlier point the Courtney character in *Kill the Moon* was called 'Emma' (Peter Harness, Twitter conversation).

It might be considered significant in this context – might, in fact, back up Danny's view by suggesting the Doctor suffers from what we might call 'rank prejudice' when it comes to the military men and women he encounters – that the older Lethbridge-Stewart was a senior officer rather than, like Danny, a mere sergeant[64]. However, Journey Blue is a lieutenant and her uncle, Morgan Blue, a colonel; the Doctor is also notably contemptuous towards the UNIT officer Colonel Ahmed, dismissing him as 'military' in exactly the same way he has Danny, confirming that his prejudice is against the armed forces in general, rather than enlisted soldiers[65]. The obvious conclusion – from our previous knowledge of the Brigadier, if not necessarily from the 2014 episodes – is that it is not his rank but the shared history and friendship between the two, going back to the Doctor's second incarnation in the late 1960s, that leads the Doctor to exempt Kate's father from his habitual view of soldiers.

This does not invalidate the distinction Danny makes, though. Because of the prevalence of class discrimination in British society, there has traditionally been a much stronger cultural divide in the British army than in some others between the 'officers' (of lieutenant rank and above) and the 'men', including non-commissioned officers up to the rank of sergeant major. While the Doctor's coding in relation to the British class hierarchy has been ambivalent during the 21st century (with Eccleston's Doctor in particular affecting a working-class accent and manner), the 20th-century Doctors were resolutely patrician in their demeanour, in

---

[64] *The Caretaker.*
[65] *Death in Heaven.* Of these, only Colonel Blue is both an officer **and** white, but the Doctor is reassuringly rude to him.

keeping with an individual carrying the hereditary title of 'Time Lord'. The terminology of this distinction allows the season to question not only whether the Doctor is 'good', but whether he is, in the military sense, a 'man'.

And indeed, the Doctor is repeatedly identified as an officer in *Death in Heaven*. When he meets Colonel Ahmed, he has already been inducted by emergency protocols into office as the President of Earth: 'the **commander-in-chief** of every army on Earth [...] the chief executive **officer** of the human race' (emphasis mine). The undead, Cyber-converted Danny calls him a 'blood-soaked old general'. And Missy offers him control of a Cyber-army with which to enforce his orders across the universe – the ultimate command position. From her unorthodox moral viewpoint, the distinction between 'good man' and bad officer is a permeable one: 'Give a good man firepower, and he'll never run out of people to kill.'

In response to Missy's offer, many of the earlier scenes discussed above are revisited in flashback, edited together to represent the Doctor's reaction to this temptation[66]:

> MISSY [in the present]

> What's the matter, Mr President? Don't you trust yourself?

> DOCTOR [from *Into the Dalek*]

> Tell me, am I a good man?

---

[66] Starting around 41 minutes 40 seconds.

DANNY [from *The Caretaker*]

Sir!

HE SALUTES.

RUSTY [from *Into the Dalek*]

I see into your soul, Doctor. I see hatred.

DOCTOR [from *Robot of Sherwood*]

TO ROBIN HOOD:

I'm not a hero.

RUSTY [from *Into the Dalek*]

You are a good Dalek.

Man or officer, good or evil, hero or monster? Like his ninth incarnation, *Death in Heaven*'s Doctor ultimately resolves the question through joyously reclaiming a term of abuse.

'Idiot' is an insult of which this exceptionally vituperative incarnation has been especially fond. Across the season's previous 11 episodes (including *Dark Water*) he has applied it seven times[67]: to Journey Blue's comrade Ross[68], implicitly to Danny[69], to all the

---

[67] For comparison, by my count the ninth Doctor uses it four times in 13 episodes (three times of Mickey); the 10th Doctor five times in 48 episodes (four times of Mickey); and the 11th Doctor seven times over the course of 44 episodes (Mickey does not appear). Interestingly, both times the ninth and 10th Doctors use it of someone other than Mickey, it happens in a Steven Moffat script.
[68] *Into the Dalek*.

survivors aboard the Orient Express[70], twice to Dr Skarosa[71] and twice to himself[72]; while earlier in *Death in Heaven* he uses it of any likely candidate for President of Earth, an evaluation which rebounds when he discovers who the President in fact is. At this revelatory moment, he uses it again:

> 'I am not a good man! I am not a bad man. I am not a hero. And I'm definitely not a president. And no, I'm not an officer. Do you know what I am? **I am an idiot**, with a box and a screwdriver.'

This declaration allows him to follow Marcus Aurelius' advice: rather than agonising over his moral status, he instead acts well, rejecting Missy's offer and handing command of the Cyber-army to Danny. This placing of the Earth's fate in the hands of a (common) soldier has implications for the episode's treatment of war and remembrance[73], but it is also a political gesture on the Doctor's part: a rejection of the class hierarchy represented by the military in favour of an alternative which, while not exactly democratic, at least respects the agency of the rank and file.

This solution also parallels the ninth Doctor's refusal in *The Parting of the Ways* to destroy the Daleks at the expense of slaughtering the population of 2,001st-century Earth. Both repudiate the earlier

---

[69] 'Some military idiot will try to attack it. The world is full of PE teachers.' (*The Caretaker*).
[70] *Mummy on the Orient Express*.
[71] *Dark Water*.
[72] *Listen, In the Forest of the Night*.
[73] See Chapter 3 for a fuller discussion of this.

genocide of the Daleks and Time Lords (which the ninth Doctor remembered committing, although the 12th Doctor now knows that those memories were false[74]) in favour of a more passive alternative.

To a measurable extent, then (and perhaps in the hope of repeating their success in introducing a new Doctor), this season's arc and its resolution mimic those of the Eccleston season. In *The Parting of the Ways*, the Doctor was saved from the consequences of what would have been a disastrous decision (resulting in the Earth's destruction and the Dalek Emperor's victory) by the arrival of his friend Rose, raised to godhood by Gallifreyan technology, who used her new powers to destroy the Daleks. *Death in Heaven*'s solution of placing the Cyber-army in control of its own destiny is politically distinctive, but an element of the same deus ex machina plotting survives nonetheless, when the Doctor is saved from the moral consequences of the separate decision to kill Missy by the arrival of his friend the Brigadier, raised from the dead by Cyber-technology, who uses his new powers to (apparently) destroy Missy.

In the emotional climax of the lengthy graveyard scene, the Doctor fulfils the Cyber-converted Brigadier's longstanding wish, and salutes him (the salute perhaps taking the place of the ninth Doctor and Rose's climactic kiss). The Cyberman does not return the salute (as one would a subordinate's), nor indeed salute him first (as one

---

[74] *The Day of the Doctor* retroactively undoes the genocide – hence the continuing plotline of Gallifrey's ambiguous survival (and, in retrospect, that of the Daleks) – while apparently leaving the earlier Doctors' memories of the event unaltered.

51

would a commander-in-chief), but instead nods in acknowledgement – confirming that the Doctor continues, for the moment, to stand outside the military hierarchy, neither a 'man' (good or bad) nor an officer.

By contrast, Clara's story across the 2014 season has only superficial similarities to Rose's in 2005. True, both women are placed in the position of choosing between a settled earthly existence with a boyfriend and a life exploring the universe with the Doctor, but this is also a dilemma faced by Amy Pond[75], and is present in embryo as long ago as the unsignalled departures of two of the earliest 20th-century companions, Susan and Vicki[76].

Unlike her predecessors, Clara has addressed her quandary by attempting (with determination, but ultimately unsuccessfully) to insulate Danny from the knowledge of her past and continuing association with the Doctor[77]. This, of course, is a generous way of putting it: more bluntly, she lies repeatedly to her boyfriend about the fact that she is being – albeit in a wholly non-romantic sense – unfaithful to him.

---

[75] Most explicitly in *Amy's Choice* (2010).
[76] In 'Flashpoint' (*The Dalek Invasion of Earth* episode six) and 'Horse of Destruction' (*The Myth Makers* episode four, 1965) respectively – although neither woman originated on contemporary Earth, or indeed ended up there. (Jon Arnold points out that the departure of Ian and Barbara also fits this pattern, on the assumption that the teachers leave the Doctor to settle down together on contemporary Earth.)
[77] In *The Caretaker*, and subsequently *Mummy on the Orient Express*, *Flatline* and *In the Forest of the Night*.

It is a characteristic solution for this season's Clara, although this is not an aspect of her personality that has been prominent previously: if anything, her character keynote has been her care for children, which has led her to work as a nanny, a parent-surrogate and most recently, a teacher. During the 2014 season, though, we have seen Clara lie many times: claiming to have had a 'skyship' encounter similar to the Sheriff of Nottingham's[78], promising Maisie that the Doctor can save her from the Foretold[79], insisting to much of the population of Bristol that she works for MI5[80], convincing the young Doctor that her presence under his bed is a dream[81], promising her present Doctor that Danny is happy for her to continue their friendship[82], and finally assuring him that nothing is wrong ('Same old same old') before ruthlessly betraying that same friendship.

The Doctor's method of containing this betrayal – using the hypnotic sleep patch on Clara to induce a hallucinatory dream-state in which she believes she is blackmailing him by throwing his TARDIS keys into an erupting volcano – is also, of course, a deception of impressive scope[83]. As River Song would remind us, the Doctor also lies[84]. Later in *Dark Water*, he demonstrates a more

---

[78] *Robot of Sherwood.*
[79] *Mummy on the Orient Express.*
[80] *Flatline.*
[81] *Listen.*
[82] *Flatline.*
[83] *Dark Water.*
[84] 'Rule One: The Doctor lies' (*The Big Bang, The Wedding of River Song*). In *Let's Kill Hitler*, we learn that she first heard this rule from the Doctor himself.

habitual technique, using his psychic paper to persuade Dr Chang that he is a government inspector. This highlights another character point for Clara, which is that she is becoming more and more like the Doctor. In *Into the Dalek*, she introduces herself as his 'carer', the Doctor blackly joking, 'She cares so I don't have to,' but this distinction has been eroded during the season. This is explored particularly in Jamie Mathieson's scripts, *Mummy on the Orient Express* and *Flatline* (and will reach its conclusion in *Face the Raven* (2015) and *Hell Bent*, in the first of which a character from *Flatline* reappears[85]).

Her first line in *Mummy on the Orient Express* is a lie ('Wonderful' on arriving on the train), to which the Doctor replies, 'The baggage car. But thanks for lying'. Ultimately we learn that the Doctor has misled Clara to bring her there, knowing that this would be no 'relaxing break' but a potentially deadly situation. The falsehood Clara later tells Maisie is on the Doctor's behalf, and she complains that he has 'made me lie. You've made me your accomplice.' By the end of he episode, though, she is deceiving him out of sheer self-interest, Insisting that Danny is 'fine with the idea of me and you knocking about.'

In *Flatline*, the Doctor discovers this deception and approves, commenting that lying is 'a vital survival skill'. This episode requires her to go further, making her the Doctor's proxy as he is stuck in the shrinking TARDIS: though relying on the MI5 cover story, she

---

[85] Notably, *Hell Bent* sees Clara lying to the Doctor (in a café, no less) throughout the framing sequence, after recapitulating the Doctor's origin story by running away from Gallifrey with a companion in a stolen TARDIS.

introduces herself as 'the Doctor [...] Dr Oswald,' and imitates the Doctor's habits and methods, causing the real Doctor to suggest that she is a doctor 'of lies'. Their final exchange in the episode returns to the 'good man' question, acknowledging that being the Doctor is a different thing from being good:

CLARA

Come on, why can't you say it? I was the Doctor and I was good.

DOCTOR

You were an exceptional Doctor, Clara.

CLARA

Thank you.

DOCTOR

Goodness had nothing to do with it.[86]

These tendencies of Clara's come to a head at the beginning of *Death in Heaven*, as she endeavours to persuade the Cybermen that she is, in fact, the Doctor, her identity as Clara being a cover story. This twist – made more plausible to us, the audience, by Moffat's tendency towards complex time-travel plotting, the previous year's multiple-Doctor stories and the still-fresh revelation of Missy's gender swap – is given credence in a bravura piece of television[87], as *Death in Heaven*'s opening credits are amended to

---

[86] The Doctor's final line here quotes a famous piece of dialogue of Mae West's (*Night after Night*, 1932).
[87] Or an irritating gimmick, depending on taste.

55

corroborate the lie, placing Jenna Coleman's name ahead of Capaldi's and her animated eyes in place of his. Not only does the Doctor lie: on occasion, **Doctor Who** does too.

In the event, Clara's deception falls apart – ironically as she insists, 'Ask anyone who knows me, I'm a brilliant liar' – and the Danny Cyberman intervenes to protect her from his more effectively converted brethren. Clara fails both as a liar and as the Doctor – perhaps because she remains, despite her best efforts, a good (wo)man – but a more stringent test is to come.

In the episode's coda in the café, Clara insists to the Doctor that Danny has returned to her, even while he maintains that the co-ordinates Missy provided have led him home to Gallifrey. Then they join together in an embrace whose symmetry matches their comforting mutual deception. As they hold each other Clara asks:

CLARA

Why don't you like hugging, Doctor?

DOCTOR

Never trust a hug. It's just a way to hide your face.

Thus both succeed in keeping their heartbreak private, and convince the other that they are happy. In the end, Clara proves herself as good a liar as the Doctor himself, and the two part as equals.

The fate of Gallifrey aside, the only obvious ongoing plot strand which survives from the 11th Doctor's tenure through to *Dark Water / Death in Heaven* is the identity of the woman who gave Clara the Doctor's phone number, as reported in *The Bells of Saint*

John[88]. The remaining flashbacks in *Death in Heaven*[89] are to the phone call itself – in which Clara explains that 'the woman in the shop' wrote it down as a helpline number – and to the Doctor's speculation in *Deep Breath* that the same person had placed an advert aimed at keeping them together.

This is an element whose resolution in *Death in Heaven* is admittedly less than elegant. Missy justifies her revelation that she was the woman responsible for introducing the Doctor to Clara as follows:

> ''Cause she's perfect, innit? The control freak and the man who should never be controlled. You'd go to hell if she asked. And she would.'

Missy's claimed intention, then, was that Clara would, one day, lead the Doctor to 3W and set in train her plan to give him a Cyber-army as a birthday present. The obvious objection to this – that Clara, who actually met 'the woman in the shop', fails to recognise Missy at the 3W facility – can be explained by the Master's long history of disguise, but it remains unconvincing in several other respects.

To begin with, it relies on Missy having some way to ensure that Clara would have a romantic partner who predeceased her, after

---

[88] Although *Deep Breath* raises a question with its origins in *The Fires of Pompeii* (2008) and its answer withheld until *The Girl Who Died* (2015); and *The Zygon Invasion / The Zygon Inversion* reveals that the events of *The Day of the Doctor* had more repercussions than was apparent at the time.
[89] Beginning around 28 minutes 45 seconds.

Missy had set up 3W as a going concern[90]. This suggests that Missy likely arranged for Danny's death shortly before the Doctor's birthday[91], having perhaps put him in the way of becoming Clara's boyfriend in the first place.

While over-elaborate plans and traps have certainly been characteristic of the Master in the past, this one relies on a cavalier confidence in the predictability of Clara's and the Doctor's behaviour which is difficult to justify. Clara's attempt to manipulate the Doctor through blackmail in *Dark Water* is explicitly a struggle for control, but prior to this story the audience could have been forgiven for not having realised that she was a control freak (just as before this season they might not have seen her as a habitual liar)[92]. Her lying to Danny could be seen as a controlling behaviour, but it seems aimed at keeping her lives with Danny and the Doctor safely compartmentalised, so as to avoid the reaction of a

---

[90] The discovery of 3W's existence is in itself a somewhat awkward piece of plotting. It clearly exists in Clara's immediate present (as Danny's body is still being held in a mortuary), and has been around for long enough to attract UNIT's attention. *Death in Heaven* suggests that knowledge has been confined to 'the super-rich', but it scarcely seems plausible that a discovery like Dr Skarosa's and a service like 3W's could exist in the world where Clara lives and works without her becoming aware of it.

[91] This undermines Clara's bleak acceptance that Danny's death was 'boring [...] ordinary' (*Dark Water*), which is perhaps one reason why it is not made explicit.

[92] She is described as a 'control freak' in both *The Time of the Doctor* (by herself, under the influence of Christmas's truth field) and *Deep Breath* (by the Doctor), but in both cases without context to corroborate the judgement.

58

boyfriend who disapproves of the company she keeps. This seems less characteristic of a control freak than of someone who fears the reaction of an abusive partner. Certainly, it is not Clara who comes off as the control freak in this exchange:

DANNY

If he ever pushes you too far, I want you to tell me, because I know what that's like. You'll tell me if that happens, yeah?

CLARA

Yeah, it's a deal.

DANNY

No. It's a promise.

CLARA

Okay. I promise.

DANNY

And if you break that promise, Clara, we're finished.

CLARA

Don't say that.

DANNY

I'm saying it because if you don't tell me the truth, I can't help you. And I could never stand not being able to help you. We clear?

CLARA

Yes. We're clear.

[*The Caretaker*]

Some viewers have read the relationship accordingly[93].

Missy has Clara pigeonholed, though, and events do indeed unfold as she expected. That this may be more due to luck than judgement is shown by the fact that Danny himself manages, almost uniquely, to override Cyber-conversion to protect his girlfriend[94], meaning that the ultimate failure of Missy's plan is caused precisely by a failure on her part to judge character and predict behaviour.

At this point we might reasonably observe that the 2015 season gives an entirely different explanation for Missy's matchmaking, which would make the Nethersphere ploy at most a test of how far the Doctor will go under Clara's influence[95]. Alternatively, we might

---

[93] See Martin, Dan, 'Doctor Who recap: Series 34, episode 9 – *Flatline*'; and 'Manipulative boyfriends vote Danny Pink best **Doctor Who** companion' – a satirical article from the *Daily Mash*, but one which presumably reflects the satirist's perception of the character.
[94] The only fully converted Cyberman seen previously in the TV series to have overridden their conditioning is Yvonne Hartman, the head of Torchwood London, in *Doomsday*.
[95] 'This is why I gave her to you in the first place, to make you see. The friend inside the enemy, the enemy inside the friend?' (*The Witch's Familiar*). Admittedly Danny's presence inside the Cyberman casing (like Clara's inside a Dalek in both *The Witch's*

well conclude that Missy acts mostly on impulse, and will opportunistically claim that any outcome that emerges is what she planned all along.

In any case, that such an apparently simple question is answered in such a convoluted and unsatisfactory way, and in a perfunctory minute of screen time (around a quarter of it spent reminding us that there was any issue to be resolved at all) is one of the few signs in *Dark Water / Death in Heaven* of the messy plotting and rushed resolution that characterised the previous year's climactic episodes[96].

Meanwhile, Danny has his own character arc, independent of his roles as Clara's dupe, Missy's victim and the butt of the Doctor's disapproval. Thanks to time-travel in *Listen* and flashbacks in *Dark Water*, we have sampled his life from childhood to his early death, including his adult career as a soldier and then a teacher.

Although the Doctor is (and apparently remains) unaware of it, Danny's decision to pursue the former career is in part the Time Lord's own responsibility. After meeting Rupert Pink as a terrified child, Clara comforts him with a story about one of his toys, 'a soldier so brave he doesn't need a gun', clearly modelled on her view of the Doctor. The Doctor telepathically grants young Rupert a

---

Familiar and her debut story *Asylum of the Daleks* (2012)) could be seen as an illustration of this.

[96] One might indeed speculate that a different revelation of the woman's identity was originally planned, although given the plethora of enigmatic manipulative women in Moffat's **Doctor Who** stories it is hard to guess exactly who this would have been.

dream of being this 'Dan the soldier man', a destiny he grows up to fulfil[97]. Without downplaying the significance of Danny's own choices, this would seem to be one lie of the Doctor's which proves true in the long run.

Danny's conscious reasons defy the Doctor's prejudices, though, by being thoughtful and at least partially altruistic: 'There's a bit more to modern soldiering than just shooting people. I like to think there's a moral dimension.' Clara's decision to date him despite her initial distaste for his previous career is in part a defiant reaction to the Doctor's refusal to accept Journey Blue as a companion precisely because she is a soldier[98].

Danny's defensiveness about his military past is established well before he meets the Doctor in *The Caretaker* and is obliged to defend himself from actual attacks on the subject. Like the ninth Doctor – a parallel which may be significant – he struggles to overcome the unresolved guilt and trauma in his past. Asked by the boy Fleming[99], 'Have you ever killed anyone who wasn't a soldier?', he responds with evasion and involuntary tears, and he refutes with more than necessary vehemence Mr Armitage's jocular charge of being 'a bit of a ladykiller'[100]. On their first date Clara jokes about him killing a pupil, and provokes an angry reaction: 'I dug 23 wells. [...] When I was a soldier. 23. [...] So why doesn't that ever get

---

[97] *Listen.*
[98] *Into the Dalek.*
[99] The cadet who is credited as appearing in *Dark Water* but does not.
[100] *Into the Dalek.*

mentioned?'[101] In *Kill the Moon* (2014), he alludes to a 'really bad day' after which he left the army[102]. As with the ninth Doctor, the likely reasons for his suppressed distress are not difficult to decode, and it is confirmed in the flashbacks in *Dark Water* that he bitterly regrets accidentally killing a civilian, an adolescent boy[103].

Danny's specific decision to become a teacher after leaving the army is fitting, given his victim's age and his own troubled past as a child in care. It also fits the prominence of children in the 2014 season, to a degree that is unusual even for Moffat's era of **Doctor Who**[104]. Partly this is due to the choice of Coal Hill School as Clara's home territory from *The Day of the Doctor* onwards (and thus a result of her character being called to care for children), but neither *The Day of the Doctor* nor the 2015 season feature children as prominently[105]. Coal Hill pupils are seen in *Deep Breath, Into the Dalek, Listen, The Caretaker, Kill the Moon* and *In the Forest of the*

---

[101] *Listen.*

[102] *Kill the Moon.*

[103] Not a lady, though, which might suggest that this is not the only civilian death which weighs on his conscience.

[104] A few of the many examples of Moffat's frequent use of children as viewpoint characters are young Reinette in *The Girl in the Fireplace*, CAL in *Silence in the Library / Forest of the Dead* and Lily and Cyril in *The Doctor, the Widow and the Wardrobe* (2011).

[105] Clara's class appears at the beginning of *The Day of the Doctor*, and the deaths of Gallifreyan children in the Time War become an important moral touchstone. In the 2015 season, Clara's class once again appears at the beginning of *The Magician's Apprentice*; there are children in *The Zygon Invasion* (although two of them turn out to be adult Zygon commanders); and non-speaking Gallifreyan children again need to be protected in *Hell Bent*.

Night[106]. *Kill the Moon*, as well as giving the rebellious schoolgirl Courtney a short-term companion role, revolves around the value of the life of a newborn creature, while *Listen* contains the only appearance to date of the Doctor himself as a child[107].

Danny's commitment to the children he teaches is clear throughout the season, but it comes especially to the fore in *In the Forest of the Night*, where he consistently prioritises his immediate duty of care over the threat to the world and his own chance of escaping it. It is in this relationship that his own credentials as 'a good man' are most clearly showcased: as already noted, his concern for Clara (however sympathetically played by Samuel Anderson) can be seen in a rather different light.

While his leadership of the Cyber-army in an act of mass self-sacrifice is portrayed as the ultimate expression of his desire to protect Clara, he commits one final act of care to a child **after** this second death, redeeming the wrong he inflicted as a soldier by restoring his young victim to life, though it means he himself cannot return from the afterlife. This resolves – in a dramatic sense – the issue of his unhappy past (as a child in need of rescue as well

---

[106] And seemingly were also filmed for *Dark Water*, if Bradley Ford's credit is anything to go by.

[107] During Moffat's time as showrunner it has become routine for us to encounter his central characters as children. Aside from the Doctor and Danny in *Listen*, we see young Amy in *The Eleventh Hour* and *The Big Bang*; young River in *Day of the Moon* (2011) and *A Good Man Goes to War* (she, Amy and Rory are also seen as teenagers in *Let's Kill Hitler*); young Clara in 'The Bells of Saint John: A Prequel' and *The Rings of Akhaten* (both 2013); and even young Davros in *The Magician's Apprentice* / *The Witch's Familiar*.

as a soldier who endangered a child), in a way which draws clearly on what we know of his present. Though somewhat diluted by Danny's reappearance in Clara's dream in *Last Christmas* (2014), it is another neat resolution of a regular's character thread...

...Or would be, except that it leaves a significant loose end dangling in the form of Colonel Orson Pink. Messily, while *Listen* supplies an essential plot mechanism for *Dark Water* – the telepathic interface in the TARDIS which allows Clara to direct it to follow Danny's timeline even beyond death – it introduces another plot element which appears to contradict it.

The clear implication of the arrival in *Listen* of a character from the future played by Anderson, bearing Danny's surname and owning one of his treasured childhood toys, is that Danny will survive to have descendants of his own. Scarcely less explicit is the implication – in Orson's half-recognition of Clara, his memory of a great-grandparent telling 'silly stories' about time-travel, and the Doctor's insistence that there must be 'some connection' between the two – that those descendants will also be Clara's. However, failing some mechanism restoring Danny to life in a future story, *Dark Water / Death in Heaven* would appear to make such a lineage impossible[108].

---

[108] Several alternative possibilities – including the obvious one at the time, that Clara is already pregnant in *Dark Water* – are ruled out by subsequent stories. Her final appearance (at time of writing) in *Hell Bent* does leave her in command of a functioning TARDIS, and thus able to visit Danny prior to his death if she so wished, but in an artificial semi-undead state in which it seems unlikely she could conceive or sustain a pregnancy.

Steven Moffat has suggested that at some point after *Death in Heaven* Clara might make contact with Danny's relatives, telling them of his sacrifice and passing them his soldier toy, and that Orson might thus be descended from another branch of the family[109]. The fact that the young Danny is in state care might make this seem unlikely, but there is nothing to suggest that he is actually an orphan: indeed, the same episode that visits the care home and introduces Orson sees Danny plead 'family stuff' as an excuse for delaying his first date with Clara[110]. Moffat's explanation might explain the physical resemblance (at least within the conventions of **Doctor Who** casting, where identical cousins are not unknown[111]), but not Orson's connection with Clara, or his belief that time-travel 'runs in the family'. Danny, after all, has never time-travelled, to our knowledge.

While only going into detail in this respect, however, Moffat says that he 'can think of several explanations'. The most obvious is perhaps that for *Listen*'s purposes Danny and Clara **do** have children together, and that Orson **is** their great-grandson; but that Missy changes this established history in *Dark Water* when she has Danny killed. This would mean that the Doctor is categorically wrong when he tells Clara that time can only be rewritten 'with great care, and not today': the timeline he is so zealous to preserve

---

[109] Moffat, Steven, 'Steven Moffat', *Doctor Who Magazine* (DWM) #481.

[110] *Listen*. On a first viewing one might suspect that Danny is lying to Clara and has some other reason to put off the date, but nothing in the later treatment of the character supports this.

[111] See *Smith and Jones* (2007).

66

is already a changed one, as he would realise had he paid more attention to the humans surrounding him[112]. By this interpretation, Orson is as much a casualty of Missy's plotting as Chang or Osgood, erased from history in a paradox as life-denying as the one the Doctor believes he is avoiding.

Aside from the Doctor, Clara, Danny and Missy, the season's regulars, the semi-regular character who receives the most development in *Dark Water / Death in Heaven* must be the timorous and self-conscious Osgood, who finds reserves of bravery to face Missy and so impresses the Doctor with her intelligence that he offers her the chance to be a companion that he withheld from Journey Blue. (Osgood, of course, is a scientist and not a solder; she may work with soldiers, but then so does the Doctor.) Unfortunately, she – **this** Osgood, at least – has made the mistake of impressing him in Missy's hearing, and pays a fatal price for it[113].

This might have been expected to curtail her character development, but in fact it will become unexpectedly relevant in *The Zygon Invasion / The Zygon Inversion*, which reveals that – while the Osgood killed by Missy is definitively dead – she was only one of a pair, one of them the original human woman and the

---

[112] Danny is no master of disguise, and Clara recognises Orson instantly despite his beard. The fact that the Doctor, having met Orson and knowing his unusual surname, apparently fails to recognise Danny as his relative in *The Caretaker* suggests considerable self-absorption on his part.

[113] *Death in Heaven*. This happens aboard the presidential plane, suggesting an alternative, subsidiary meaning for the episode's title.

67

other the Zygon duplicate from *The Day of the Doctor*. The surviving Osgood is, more than ever, daring, resourceful and cool under pressure, and at the end of the 2015 two-parter the Doctor will reiterate his offer. Osgood, though, will turn him down on the grounds that Earth needs her ambivalent identity as a symbol of the human-Zygon accord. (Whether this borderline messiah complex on the part of a formerly diffident woman is organic character development or the result of the Zygon duplicate forgetting certain key details of its original's personality, is perhaps a matter of interpretation.)

Of the remaining recurring cast, Clara's Gran from *The Time of the Doctor* appears in only a single scene (where her behaviour is, reasonably enough, more suited to visiting a grieving relative than flirting with strange men at a boozy Christmas lunch); Seb has appeared in only one previous scene, in which his behaviour was identically smug and corporate; and Mr Armitage contributes only a voiceover. This leaves us with Kate Stewart to consider.

From her first appearance, Kate's character has been largely defined in relation to her father: though undeniably portrayed as a competent woman in her own right, a scientist and a leader of the UNIT military (without being herself a soldier), outside this function her personality in *The Power of Three* and *The Day of the Doctor* has largely consisted of living up to her late father's expectations, and to the Doctor's expectations of her father's daughter[114]. Her

---

[114] We can also say that she has an admirable concern for the fate of humanity at large, a pride in her job, a protective concern for her subordinates and a dry sense of humour, but most of this would fall under the above rubric.

68

unnecessarily lengthy catalogue of her own personality traits when introducing herself ('Divorcee, mother-of-two, keen gardener, outstanding bridge player; also Chief Scientific Officer, Unified Intelligence Taskforce...'[115]) feels almost plaintive. Despite a fine performance by Jemma Redgrave, on her third appearance the character remains in the shadow of her more famous father, a reliable anchor for the Doctor during two decades of televised **Doctor Who**[116].

The inequality of this relationship, at least for those aware of the momentum of the Lethbridge-Stewart continuity juggernaut, gives Kate's father's brief, non-speaking appearance as one of the Cyber-resurrected dead an importance which threatens to outweigh her extensive speaking part.

In the event, that weight is rather more than said appearance will bear. As well as a fan-pleasing gesture (although it inevitably failed to please all fans [117]), the Cyber-Brigadier's brief, silent

---

[115] *Death in Heaven.*
[116] Although the character appeared only five times after 1975, his lengthy (and continuing) afterlife in tie-in media, and the actor's ubiquity at **Doctor Who** conventions prior to his illness, helped to cement this impression among fans.
[117] See, for instance, Burns, Stuart Ian, 'Death in Heaven':
'The cyberfication of Alistair is tasteless isn't it? Having given the much loved character a decent send off in *The Wedding of River Song* and respectfully resurrected his spirit in Kate [...] we now have his spirit encased in a flying Cyberman [...] the whole idea of it, and the business of the salute is just horrendous.'

appearance [118] serves to eliminate Missy (for immediate plot purposes); to save Kate from death (for ongoing storyline purposes); to give Kate some emotional closure (although we are only told by Clara that 'she's talking about her Dad', rather than hearing it); to continue the theme of military remembrance (beyond, perhaps, what might seem to be its reasonable endpoint)[119]; and to affirm (in his willingness to salute his friend) that the Doctor has overcome at least some of his aversion to the military[120]. To achieve all this with such a minimalist cameo is difficult, and the scene does not wholly succeed.

Certainly the moment is insufficiently foreshadowed, with the Doctor's brief exchange with Kate in front of her father's portrait the viewer's only preparation for the return of a character who many of them will have never seen, unless they remember a **Sarah Jane Adventures** story from six years previously[121]. That Nicholas Courtney was unavailable to reprise his performance is, of course, unavoidable, but it would at least have allowed his character to be recognised from the portrait. It would also have circumvented the cognitive dissonance of the scene (in which our attention is counterproductively focused on the identity of the actor wearing the Cyberman suit), and what some have seen as the dubious taste

---

[118] Slightly over a minute elapses between the first evidence of the Cyber-Brigadier's presence (the beam that vaporises Missy) and his disappearance into the skies.
[119] For an interesting ramification of this, see Chapter 3.
[120] Certainly he manages to cooperate with UNIT without being excessively insulting in *The Zygon Invasion / The Zygon Inversion*.
[121] Although DVDs and downloads of both these stories, and nearly all the others featuring Lethbridge-Stewart, do of course exist.

of bringing back a deceased actor's character as a literal walking corpse[122].

It may be significant, however, that in Kate's appearances in 2015, from *The Magician's Apprentice* onward, her more famous father is not mentioned and the character is allowed to stand in her own right without constant comparisons being made. Possibly, for the sake of her long-term character, the Brigadier had to appear as a revenant so his ghost could be exorcised.

The final plot thread to be considered belongs to a character appearing here for the first time. Nick Frost's manifestation as Santa Claus during the closing credits of *Death in Heaven* lasts a mere 30 seconds, and on the face of it exists simply to trail the Christmas special, *Last Christmas* – as the arrival of Catherine Tate in a wedding dress did for *The Runaway Bride* in 2006[123], and that of the Titanic through the TARDIS console room wall for *Voyage of the Damned* in 2007[124].

Unlike either of these scenes, however, Santa's appearance here does not lead directly into *Last Christmas*, for all that that episode features him heavily. In the Christmas story, Santa and the Doctor arrive separately on Clara's roof on Christmas Eve, and neither makes reference to any earlier meeting. Quite aside the fact that *Last Christmas* is, at least until its final two minutes, a long

---

[122] Though far less blatantly so than the Master's earlier return as a skull-faced ghoul in *The Deadly Assassin* (1976) only three years after Roger Delgado's death in 1973.
[123] *Doomsday.*
[124] *Last of the Time Lords.*

71

sequence of nested dream sequences[125], this calls into question the experiential value of Santa's presence in the TARDIS.

Indeed, the fact that the vignette begins with the Doctor apparently asleep suggests that from his point of view within the fiction this, too, is a dream (the second in the two-parter, after the sleep-patch hallucination he imposed on Clara in *Dark Water*). From our point of view, its placement within the end credits – the first such interpolation in **Doctor Who**'s long history – locates the sequence in a similarly liminal space, part neither of the drama we have been watching nor of the facts about its production.

Appropriately, then – whether he is a manifestation of the fictional Doctor's subconscious mind or a metafictional commentary on the action – Santa's dialogue acts as a critique of the preceding adventure, and its conclusion in particular[126]:

> 'You know it can't end like that. Mm? We need to get this sorted, and quickly. She's not all right, you know. And neither are you.'

---

[125] The status of these final two minutes remains ambivalent: the presence of the tangerine may suggest either that Santa is, indeed, real, or that the Doctor and Clara remain in a dream. The implications of the latter mean that it should probably be considered unlikely, at least in the context of the Doctor's continuing narrative.

[126] Interestingly, Moffat's Children in Need special 'Time Crash' (2007) – taking place at a similarly liminal point between onscreen scenes, after Martha's exit in *Last of the Time Lords* but before the *Titanic*'s arrival immediately thereafter – also develops into a commentary on **Doctor Who**, as David Tennant's 10th Doctor waxes nostalgic about the fifth Doctor's era.

72

The natural assumption is that Santa is referring here to Clara, who we have just seen the Doctor part with – though if this is a dream, this suggests that the Doctor, at least, is aware (though perhaps subconsciously) of their mutual deception in the cafe. Given the interdependence between the two Time Lords, though, Santa's admonition could also relate to Missy – and as Clara will point out in *The Magician's Apprentice*, by the next season the Doctor either knows or hopes that his old friend has survived.

Despite his dubious ontological status here, though, Santa's identity as a trusted figure of childhood belief – a kind, elderly, white-bearded figure easily confused with God, as young Amelia Pond does in *The Eleventh Hour* (2010) – means that we believe his judgement implicitly. Clara (or Missy, as the case may be) has unfinished business with the Doctor. She will be back. The implicit promise of 'What do you want for Christmas?' – in context a barely disguised reminder of the upcoming seasonal episode – benefits from the same authority.

Unlike the deliberately surreal non-sequiturs which end *Doomsday* and *Last of the Time Lords*, Santa's appearance has a real connection with what precedes it as well as what comes after, acting as a link in a chain rather than a conceptual jump-cut. It also acts as the capstone to a running theme of the 2014 season.

The 12th Doctor's first year has presented us (in episodes which are not ostensibly dream-sequences, although they sometimes use dreamlike imagery) with Robin Hood and his Merry Men[127]; a

---

[127] *Robot of Sherwood.*

dragon hatching from an egg that is the Moon[128]; an undead mummy implacably pursuing the living[129]; a magical forest where a red-coated girl flees from wolves and fairies return lost children to their parents[130]; and – finally – ghosts, Heaven and the resurrection of the dead. More than any previous year of **Doctor Who**, 2014 has asked us to believe that stories, myths and legends can be true[131]. It seems entirely fitting that the same year's Christmas episode should feature the literal spirit of Christmas in a starring role, even if his objective existence remains ambiguous and questionable.

It is also fitting that he is included in *Dark Water / Death in Heaven*, as it, too, is a seasonal episode, of a kind **Doctor Who** has never previously attempted.

---

[128] *Kill the Moon.*
[129] *Mummy on the Orient Express.*
[130] *In the Forest of the Night.*
[131] Alternatively, Alan Stevens suggests that *Last Christmas* may imply that they are all a dream.

CHAPTER 3. 'THE ARMY OF THE DEAD': THE SEASONAL SPECIAL

Dark Water was first broadcast on 1 November 2014, the day after Halloween. *Death in Heaven* was broadcast a week later on 8 November, the day before Remembrance Sunday. These dates contribute to the characters of the individual episodes, and to the overall flavour of the two-part story, in ways which have previously been seen in **Doctor Who** only with Christmas and anniversary stories.

Dark Water is a ghost story, a tale of post-mortem communication and animate skeletons with a horrific conceit at its centre, while *Death in Heaven* is an elegiac story of mourning and self-sacrifice, and of the heroism of the dead. As these are two halves of a single story, however, elements of both celebrations – which in any case overlap in images of graves and in a heightened concentration on the dead – permeate both episodes.

Halloween is a modern secular interpretation of All Hallows' Eve, the evening preceding All Hallows' Day or All Saints' Day on 1 November. This is itself a Christian updating of the earlier pagan festival of Samhain which marked the beginning of winter and of the Celtic year, when the dead were thought to be more than usually supernaturally active in the world[132]. These days Halloween

---

[132] According, at least, to a leaflet issued by the British Pagan Federation in 1993, and quoted in Hutton, Ronald, *The Stations of the Sun*, p360. While Professor Hutton goes on to question the precision of some of the Federation's assertions, he does not

is distinguished primarily by costumed children (often but not invariably dressed in grotesque horror-movie style) calling door-to-door to demand sweets from acquaintances and strangers, and the occasional party for grown-ups involving similar costumes; but the original concept survives in Britain in the established Anglican church's prayers for the dead and in an increasing awareness of the more colourful celebrations of other global cultures, notably the Mexican Day of the Dead[133].

Remembrance Sunday is also a festival of the Anglican church, occurring on the second Sunday in November. It takes its name and character from its proximity to 11 November, Remembrance Day proper (known in some countries as Armistice Day or Veterans' Day), the anniversary of the armistice which ended the First World War in 1918. In the UK during the period surrounding Remembrance Day, the war dead are honoured by wreath-laying ceremonies at local and national war memorials, a two minutes' silence at 11am on 11 November, and the wearing of artificial poppies distributed by the nation's highest-profile charity, the Royal British Legion.

Obviously it is a coincidence that these dates fall so closely together, as none of the signatories to the 1918 armistice can have had such a thing in mind. Still, while Remembrance Day would have

---

dispute that this is the popular interpretation of Samhain among non-specialists (even those who observe it religiously).

[133] Itself an updating of a Native American tradition, moved by colonial authorities to fall in line with the Catholic ecclesiastical calendar.

76

been concerned with commemorating millions of deaths whenever it came in the year, that it takes place early in November is peculiarly appropriate. Like Samhain and its successor festivals, it falls during the autumn when – in the northern European agricultural calendar, at least – crops have been harvested, animals slaughtered, vegetation is dying back and thoughts are on survival through the winter. A melancholy, funereal atmosphere and a mood of sombre recollection are the order of the season. While little awareness of this tradition may survive among modern, and especially young and urban, TV audiences, autumn can nevertheless be a depressing time for them too, when evenings become darker, days shorter and the inclement weather increasingly forces them indoors for the duration of winter.

It was also, during much of the programme's history, part of the traditional season for watching **Doctor Who**. *Deep Breath*'s broadcast on 23 August 2014 was the first time since 1989 that an entire season of **Doctor Who** had been broadcast at this time of year, but during the 20th century the series' episodes tended to cluster in the darker months of the year, and September was the most common month for a new season to begin. The revived series, by contrast, began by appearing routinely in spring, and prior to 2011 only one full-length episode of the 21st-century series – the one-off *The Waters of Mars* (15 November 2009) – had gone out between early July and Christmas[134].

---

[134] The 2005 and 2007 Children in Need specials, 'Born Again' and 'Time Crash', were also broadcast on 18 and 16 November in their respective years.

Only with the splitting of the 2011 and 2012-13 seasons did regular episodes start appearing in the autumn again. Steven Moffat saw this development as a matter for celebration:

> 'Everything's seasonal – even television – and that leads me to a confession: **Doctor Who** in the summer? All that running down tunnels, with torches, and the sunlight streaming through your windows and bleaching out the screen? All those barbecues and children playing outside, while on the telly there are green monsters seething in their CGI-enhanced lairs? It's just not right, is it? Be honest. For me, as a kid, when the afternoon got darker and there was a thrill of cold in the air, I knew that even though summer was over, the TARDIS was coming back!'[135]

For Moffat 'as a kid' between the ages of one and four, a new season of **Doctor Who** had started every autumn, as had six consecutive seasons in the late 1970s (making up almost the whole of the Tom Baker era) when he would have been between twelve and eighteen[136]. While the gap as he aged from five to 11 makes it clear that this was not the universal rule he seems to recall, the variation would have provided sufficient basis for him to conclude that, in resuming its autumn start in 1975, **Doctor Who** had returned to the appropriate time in the schedules. It is easy to see how 2011 would have felt to him like a similar homecoming.

---

[135] Moffat, Steven, 'Production Notes', DWM #411.

[136] Counting the end of August as 'autumn', this is true of the 1963-67 seasons (but not the 1968 season, which started as early as 10 August), and the 1975-80 seasons. Moffat was born on 18 November 1961.

78

The more specific idea of a **Doctor Who** episode tied to a particular date of broadcast appears surprisingly early in the programme's history. 'The Feast of Steven'[137] (*The Daleks' Master Plan* episode 7, 1965) was in fact the only episode to be shown on 25 December until 2005. The first part of the episode, a comedy police procedural set in contemporary Liverpool, makes several passing references to the fact that it also takes place on Christmas Day, but the festival's only direct impact on the events of the story comes at the end, as William Hartnell's Doctor salutes the viewer with a Christmas toast. Less prominently, 'Volcano' (*The Daleks' Master Plan* episode 8, 1966), broadcast a week after 'The Feast of Steven', involves a brief sequence set during the New Year's Eve celebrations at Trafalgar Square.

Such scenes were not repeated in the 20th century. The nearest thing to a **Doctor Who** Christmas special during the ensuing four decades is not a **Doctor Who** episode at all, but the pilot of the abortive **K-9 and Company** spinoff series. *A Girl's Best Friend* (1981), broadcast on 28 December and set shortly before Christmas, introduces K-9 Mark III as a Christmas present to Sarah Jane Smith from the Doctor and ends with the eponymous automaton attempting to sing 'We Wish You a Merry Christmas'. Thematically, it draws little more from the festive season than 'The Feast of Steven'.

---

[137] Although the wordplay of the title links the Doctor's companion Steven Taylor with the popular Christmas carol 'Good King Wenceslas', St Stephen's Day is in fact Boxing Day, 26 December.

79

Since the revival of the series in 2005, however, and specifically its recommissioning for a Christmas episode the same year, this particular variety of seasonal special has become a standing feature of the show. At the time of writing 11 Christmas specials have been broadcast, from *The Christmas Invasion* in 2005 to *The Husbands of River Song* in 2015, and from this body of work it is possible to draw some specific conclusions about what seasonal **Doctor Who** looks like.

Under Russell T Davies, what Christmas supplies is largely an aesthetic. His annual scripts quickly establish a pattern based on turning Christmas iconography to menacing ends: the stories feature killer robots disguised as angels or Santas, murderous animated Christmas trees, an alien warship shaped like a Christmas star. The plots are barely affected: the stories of the Sycorax invasion, the Racnoss attack, the wreck of the Titanic, the birth of the Cyberking and the return of the Time Lords could have been told and set at any time of year with minimal tinkering. As far as Davies's stories are concerned with Christmas, they see it as a time of secular celebration, when families and friends enjoy fellowship, food and the exchange of presents. In *The Christmas Invasion* the Doctor – who has previously refused to become involved in Rose's 'domestic' affairs – sits down to Christmas dinner with her, Jackie and Mickey and is for the first time accepted as part of their family. Davies repeats this motif of the Doctor's invitation to a family Christmas dinner, to somewhat diminishing effect, in *The Runaway Bride* and *The Next Doctor* (2008).

Although the Doctor jokes in *Voyage of the Damned* about having taken the last room at the inn at Bethlehem, it is only late in Davies's time as showrunner that he begins to consider the

80

season's traditional spiritual aspect. Miss Hartigan in *The Next Doctor* times the Cyberking's 'birth' for Christmas Day as a warped rejoinder to Christian sermonising, and the narrator of *The End of Time* (who will turn out to be Rassilon, the Time Lord founder and President) describes Christmas as 'the celebration of a pagan rite to banish the cold and the dark'.

The latter story deals with rebirth, as the Master is reconstituted by his followers, the Doctor regenerates and even the Time Lords return, but little effort is made to connect this with the rebirth of the year. Davies wrote to Benjamin Cook, his correspondent and co-author in *The Writer's Tale*: 'All those church bells ringing, people celebrating, out with the old and in with the new... oh that fits a dying Doctor. [...] New beginnings.' Nevertheless, his awareness of the fit seems to have been superficial: a reference in the same email to 'a Doctor born and dying on Christmas Day' turns out to relate specifically to David Tennant's first full episode as the Doctor having been *The Christmas Invasion*, rather than an understanding of the season's death-and-resurrection symbolism[138].

Davies's successor has generally paid less detailed attention to the imagery of Christmas. Although *Last Christmas* deploys the iconography of Santa Claus to great effect, Moffat's Christmas specials usually adopt the background aesthetic of the Victorian

---

[138] Davies, Russell T, and Benjamin Cook, *The Writer's Tale* p484. Jon Arnold suggests that this is can be seen as a Welsh cultural attitude, the result of an upbringing in which chapel acts as a cohesive social force even where its doctrines are seen as less important.

Christmas card (seen under Davies in *The Next Doctor* and *The Unquiet Dead* (2005), a story set but not broadcast at Christmas) and apply it not only to historical periods (in the 1890s setting of *The Snowmen* (2012) and the 1940s one of *The Doctor, The Widow and the Wardrobe*) but also to future ones (in the suspiciously Dickensian-looking colony worlds of *A Christmas Carol* (2010), *The Time of the Doctor* and *The Husbands of River Song*).

However, Moffat takes notably more interest in the thematic potential of his seasonal setting[139]. An early voiceover in *A Christmas Carol* recalls, but elaborates substantially upon, that in the previous year's *The End of Time*:

> 'On every world, wherever people are, in the deepest part of the winter, at the exact mid-point, everybody stops and turns and hugs, as if to say, well done. Well done, everyone. We're halfway out of the dark. Back on Earth, we called this Christmas, or the Winter Solstice.'

Although an atheist like Davies – and equally happy to celebrate the secular ritual of Christmas dinner[140] – Moffat has been more open to treating Christmas in metaphysical terms, as a vehicle for rebirth, rejuvenation and transformation.

A Christmas Carol returns to the Dickensian territory staked out by *The Unquiet Dead*, but recapitulates Charles Dickens' novella more

---

[139] At least until *The Husbands of River Song* (2015), where the focus is wholly on the Doctor's relationship with River and the festival is relegated to window-dressing once again.

[140] In, for instance, *The Doctor, the Widow and the Wardrobe* and *Time of the Doctor*.

closely, using time-travel to turn the misanthropic Kazran Sardick into his own spectres of Christmas Past, Present and Future, and using the metaphor of freezing and thawing (both meteorological and cryogenic) to explore his gradual change of heart. *The Snowmen* returns to this imagery in the various resurrections of Clara. *The Doctor, the Widow and the Wardrobe* treats the 'life force' of an alien forest as an autonomous entity capable of escaping its own destruction – and in the process miraculously resurrecting Madge's husband Reg – through a cosmic rebirth whose mysticism is quite atypical both of Moffat and of **Doctor Who**. *The Time of the Doctor* gives unusual emphasis to the Doctor's death and rebirth, showing him living to old age as the protective spirit of the human settlement of Christmas, and assuring Clara and us that he is beyond regeneration entirely, before his lifecycle is rebooted by the agency of the Time Lords.

In keeping with this idea of new life, the 2010s' specials often present a child's perspective on Christmas as an ideal to which adults should aspire. Moffat's abiding interest in the viewpoint of children is one of the most obvious distinctions between his and Davies's **Doctor Who**[141], and his Christmases, too, are often seen through children's eyes – young Kazran's, Cyril's and Lily's, Francesca's and Digby's, Barnable's. This may explain why Santa Claus – mentioned by Moffat in *The Doctor Dances, The Eleventh Hour* and *A Christmas Carol* – becomes a major character in *Last*

---

[141] Jackson Lake's son Frederick in Davies's *The Next Doctor* is a notable exception to this, although he plays a limited part in the action compared with Moffat's child characters such as young Kazran and the Arwell and Latimer children.

83

Christmas, effectively daring the audience to adopt a child's-eye view by accepting his existence.

So much for Christmas. We have to look harder to find examples of other seasonal celebrations receiving parallel attention in **Doctor Who**. Aside from those already mentioned, the only 20th-century stories to draw significance from their dates of broadcast were the anniversary stories *The Five Doctors* (1983) and *Silver Nemesis* (1988)[142] – and given that this significance exists outside the fiction, the texts themselves can make only coded acknowledgement of the fact. Davies's tenure as showrunner did feature a nominal Easter special, *The Planet of the Dead* (2009), but its seasonal content consists entirely of the Doctor obliquely reminiscing about having been there for 'the original' while eating a chocolate egg. The first part of Moffat's first season finale, *The Pandorica Opens*, was broadcast on 19 June and set largely at Stonehenge, but no connection is made between the story's midsummer broadcast and the ancient monument's famous alignment with the solar solstices[143].

Given **Doctor Who**'s affinity for horrific imagery, its first 50 years of stories are surprisingly neglectful of Halloween. The only 20th-century episode to go out on 31 October, 'Planet of Giants' (*Planet*

---

[142] While *The Three Doctors* opens **Doctor Who**'s 10th season, its dates of broadcast (30 December 1972 to 20 January 1973) fall far closer to the series' ninth anniversary than its 10th.

[143] Perhaps because the most significant date in story terms is 26 June 2010 – the date of *The Big Bang*'s broadcast, Amy and Rory's wedding and the destruction of the universe.

of Giants episode one, 1964) makes no mention of the date[144]; nor has any televised **Doctor Who** story to date been explicitly set at Samhain, although *The Dæmons* and *Image of the Fendahl* (1977) invoke occult significance by claiming the Celtic festival dates of Beltane and Lammas respectively[145]. Though sometimes perceived as a slightly dislocated Halloween special due to its broadcast date, *The Waters of Mars* was originally conceived as a Christmas episode, and its exact date of broadcast was unclear until very late in the writing process[146].

An argument might be made for reading *Remembrance of the Daleks* – broadcast during October 1988, but probably set in the November of 1963[147] – as a Remembrance Day story. The most obvious evidence for this is of course the title (the third in a sequence beginning with the eponymous monsters' *Resurrection* (1984) and *Revelation* (1985)), but the Second World War looms large in certain characters' backstories, and the commemoration of

---

[144] Nor does *The Zygon Invasion*, broadcast 31 October 2015.
[145] According to Professor Horner in *The Dæmons* episode 1, and Martha Tyler in *Image of the Fendahl* episode 3. Beltane (1 May) and Lammas (1 August) are the quarterly equivalents of Samhain in the Celtic pagan calendar, marking the respective beginnings of summer and autumn, while the start of spring is called Imbolc (1 February). *The Dæmons* began broadcasting three weeks after May Day, *Image of the Fendahl* not until late October.
[146] Davies and Cook, *The Writer's Tale*, pp426-28.
[147] The year is established in dialogue and in numerous supporting details; the month is based on a visible calendar and, more dubiously, on one not-quite-reference to **Doctor Who** itself, which appears to be metafictionally not-quite-suggesting that the BBC is about to broadcast an early episode of the series.

the dead (in the imagery of coffins and graveyards, and the closing funeral scene) is more prominent than is customary in **Doctor Who** of any era[148]. However, the only explicit Remembrance Day sequence in a **Doctor Who** story prior to 2014 – a brief one – comes at the end of *The Family of Blood* (2007), when Tim Latimer, seen as a boy in the 1913 setting, reappears in a coda at a contemporary memorial ceremony as an ancient, and decorated, First World War veteran[149].

It has to be admitted that nothing explicit in *Dark Water / Death in Heaven* ties the episodes to these dates either. No indication is given that any of the characters are celebrating either Halloween or Remembrance Day – indeed, the fact that nobody is wearing poppies rather suggests the opposite. While the date of a story's broadcast sometimes aligns with that of its contemporary setting, there are far too many counterexamples for us to assume that this applies as a rule. The strongest hints at the time of year come in *Death in Heaven*, in references to three separate dates.

First, the Doctor remarks, on the sudden eruption of rocket-powered Cybermen from the dome of St Paul's Cathedral, that 'Everyone in London just clapped and went "whee"[150].' This is a

---

[148] *Remembrance of the Daleks* was broadcast from 5 to 26 October 1988. Ben Aaronovitch's other TV **Doctor Who** story, *Battlefield*, is not set at Remembrance Day but does include a ceremony at a war memorial.
[149] *The Family of Blood* was broadcast on 2 June 2007. Paul Cornell's other TV **Doctor Who** story, *Father's Day* (2005), takes place in a church the day before Remembrance Sunday 1987, but the fact goes unmentioned.
[150] *Death in Heaven*.

reference to public firework displays, which – although now commonly held at other celebrations during the darker months, New Year especially – are traditionally most strongly associated in the UK with Guy Fawkes' Night, 5 November.

Secondly, Missy intends the Cyber-army to be a present for the Doctor's birthday. Within the fiction we are given no date of birth for the Doctor, and the fact that a time-traveller might personally be approaching such a milestone provides little clue as to the objective date. Nonetheless, the anniversary we most associate with the Doctor is the same date as that given for Clara's birthday – 23 November, when 'An Unearthly Child' (*An Unearthly Child* episode one, 1963) was broadcast. On this basis, weak though it is, we might assume that *Death in Heaven* takes place shortly before **Doctor Who**'s 51st birthday, 23 November 2014. (Danny twice notes the date of Clara's birthday with no suggestion that it is due shortly, but he has other things on his mind[151].)

Thirdly, when he appears in the final moments of the story, Santa Claus asks the Doctor, 'Now, stop gawping and tell me – what do you want for Christmas?' This suggests that the present-giving festival is imminent – but again this is hardly a precise dating, even disregarding the possibility that this sequence may not follow on directly from the previous scene (from which it is separated by the first few seconds of credits), and the likelihood that it is a dream sequence.

---

[151] Once when speaking to Clara from the Nethersphere in *Dark Water*, and once as a Cyberman (only later revealed to be Danny) in *Death in Heaven*.

While together these facts hint at an autumn setting, none of them is sufficiently compelling or precise to pin the action down definitively. (In this respect the story clearly differs from the Christmas specials, all of which are at least partially set explicitly on either Christmas Day or Christmas Eve.) I am not, therefore, suggesting that any of the **characters** associate the events of the story with the notable dates of early November, but that the **audience**, having these various celebrations in mind at the time of broadcast, is invited by the visuals and the content of the episodes to make this association.

This is true from the pre-credits sequence of *Dark Water*, which twice invokes Remembrance Day iconography. The opening shot is of the Welsh National War Memorial in Cardiff, a neoclassical colonnade surrounding a plinth bearing bronze statues of military personnel and an angel. Nobody in the story remarks on its presence (or the fact that it has been relocated to London for story purposes, despite bearing a prominent inscription in Welsh), but it dominates the frame for the first seconds of the episode, dwarfing Danny as he receives Clara's fatal phone call. The iconography of Remembrance Day is evoked again three minutes later when the Doctor, by contrast, is ignoring the phone call in which Clara will tell him of Danny's death: the alien landscape where the TARDIS has set down includes giant teardrop-shaped growths which, like a Remembrance Day poppy, consist of black centres surrounded by vivid red. Again, these are never mentioned, but along with the war memorial they set the tone for the episode, in which mourning for a soldier drives the protagonists' motivations and the plot.

These motifs recur throughout *Dark Water / Death in Heaven*. Part of the decor in the 3W mausoleum visited by Clara and the Doctor

88

is an obelisk of the shape common to many British war memorials. Box Cemetery in Llanelli, where much of *Death in Heaven* was filmed, contains a number of gravestones of this design: the TARDIS is placed next to one, and others are seen in different shots behind Danny and behind the Cyber-Brigadier. *Dark Water* makes repeated use of the red and black colour scheme – in, for instance, the establishing shot of the volcano; the Doctor's cape; the votive flame surmounting the largest memorial at the 3W mausoleum; the berries on Missy's hat; and the phone box standing behind Missy during the episode's climax. (Verbally, too, there are reminders of the word 'poppy' in Missy's use of the word 'pop' when killing Osgood and threatening Clara – and perhaps even in her imitation of Mary Poppins, though the name is never spoken.) The external appearance of the Matrix data-slice containing the Nethersphere inverts the poppy's colour scheme with circular red lights embedded in a black surface, just as the Nethersphere itself perverts the principles underlying Remembrance Day by conscripting the dead into further service.

Imagery reminiscent of Halloween, meanwhile, is amply supplied by the water tombs in *Dark Water*, and *Death in Heaven*'s graveyard scenes. The former are first seen soon after the Doctor and Clara arrive at the 3W mausoleum, and the image of the bones sitting upright in tanks of water, supported by unseen 'support exoskeletons', is unnerving enough even while they remain static. Barely a minute and a half later, though, these dead begin to show signs of life: first one solitary turning skull, then many, followed by reaching arms and eventually standing, animate skeletons evoking the familiar personification of death. Shortly afterwards, as the dark water which has concealed their exoskeletons drains away, they are revealed as Cybermen.

The Cybermen have been coded in various ways in their appearances in **Doctor Who**, from Wagnerian supermen to early-adopting corporate dupes[152]. One such coding casts these formerly humanlike beings, whose organic bodies are granted indefinite life by cybernetics that negate and deaden their emotions, as a new, technologically mediated form of the undead, analogous to the vampires, mummies and zombies – and the animate skeletons – of the horror genre. This identity is alluded to in their shroudlike faces in *The Tenth Planet* (1966), their association with plague in *The Moonbase* (1967) and *Revenge of the Cybermen* (1975), their first emergence from 'tombs' (in fact cryogenic chambers) in *The Tomb of the Cybermen*, their partial manifestation as 'ghosts' in *Army of Ghosts*[153] and the creeping severed Cyber-head which tries to convert Amy in *The Pandorica Opens*. Even their arbitrary vulnerabilities – radiation, gold, nail-polish remover – recall the sunlight and silver and garlic of vampire lore.

Accordingly, when the dead arise in Cyber-form in *Death in Heaven*, it is such horror tropes that are once again evoked, with disturbances in the earth in front of gravestones giving way to fingers, hands and finally entire figures emerging, transformed, into

---

[152] Respectively in *Silver Nemesis* and *Rise of the Cybermen*.
[153] This idea anticipates *Death in Heaven* without following through on its promise. It would have been notably more chilling, for instance, if the 'ghost' mistakenly identified by Jackie as her late father had in fact turned out to be his Cyber-converted alternative-universe self.

a grotesque new life. In their behaviour, the shambling disorientated figures who climb from the graves recall the zombies of modern cinema – although the fact that they have been raised as servants by a figure whom a later episode title will call a 'Witch' relates them more closely to the old-school zombie servants of traditional Haitian folklore[154].

(A further link to horror cinema, although of an entirely different vintage, occurs in *Dark Water*'s title, which it shares with a 2005 Hollywood remake of a Japanese horror film[155]. Though the film also features ominous rain and the soul of a child who died prematurely, there is little else to tie them together.)

It has to be acknowledged that such imagery is far from unusual for **Doctor Who**, and might not in itself constitute evidence of a specific Halloween tone. An 'emergence from graves' sequence was seen in *The Curse of Fenric* (1989), for instance, and walking skeletons appeared in *Silence in the Library / Forest of the Dead*. There are, indeed, examples of undead imagery earlier in the 2014 season, in the uncanny flesh-augmented clockwork robots in *Deep Breath*; in the titular *Mummy on the Orient Express*, another soldier prolonged beyond its natural life by technology; and in the jerky forms of their vivisected victims which the Boneless take on in *Flatline*. In itself, the Halloween imagery in *Dark Water / Death in*

---

[154] *The Next Doctor*, the other 21st-century Doctor Who story where a 'witch' controls Cybermen in a graveyard, makes no such connection.

[155] Also titled *Dark Water* (2002) in English, and based on a short story in a collection by Kōji Suzuki whose English title is also *Dark Water* (2004).

Heaven is less suggestive (though more prevalent) than the Remembrance Day imagery; it is in the episodes' themes that the connection becomes more clear.

The clearest sign that *Dark Water* was conceived as a Halloween episode lies in its central conceit: that the dead can speak to the living. The foundations for this were laid during Missy's earlier appearances in *Deep Breath, Into the Dalek* and *The Caretaker*, where the souls of the Half-Face Man, Gretchen Carlisle and Community Support Officer Matthew were all seen to survive their deaths, and to be welcomed by Missy or Seb to the realm variously known as Heaven, the Promised Land or the Nethersphere.

None of these episodes hinted at communication between the dead and the living, however; nor has this been a common occurrence in **Doctor Who**. While apparent 'ghosts' have been seen frequently, they are generally explained away as phenomena other than the spirits of the dead – for instance as holograms, psychic projections, gaseous beings, otherdimensional intruders or time-travellers[156]. Moffat's own *The Time of Angels / Flesh and Stone* shows the consciousness of a dead person artificially prolonged and repurposed as a communications channel[157], but actual contact with autonomous dead people has been seen unambiguously in only one previous **Doctor Who** story, *Silence in the Library / Forest of the Dead* – again by Moffat. There, as here, it is explained by the uploading of minds into a cyberspace

---

[156] See – among other examples – *The Talons of Weng-Chiang, The Awakening* (1984), *The Unquiet Dead, Army of Ghosts* and *Hide* (2013).
[157] As does the later *Under the Lake / Before the Flood* (2015).

simulation. It is only towards the end of *Dark Water*, however, that the Nethersphere is identified with 'cyberspace'; prior to this, the party line is that it is the afterlife proper, with the surprising addition of iPads explained by the arrival of the late Steve Jobs[158].

While Clara's eventual conversation with Danny is accordingly mediated by technology, not unlike a phone call with intermittent signal, the ghostly communication which Dr Chang first replays to her and the Doctor in *Dark Water* is a lot more uncanny. Chang describes it in terms aimed at destabilising and unnerving the viewer: he tells them that the truth is 'disturbing', that it might cause them to 'freak out' and that, while 'people are scared of dying [...] They'd be a lot more scared if they knew what it was really like.' He explains post-mortem communication in terms which recall 'electronic voice phenomena', a modern attempt at technologically-mediated mediumship[159]:

> 'White noise off the telly. We've all heard it. A few years ago, Doctor Skarosa, our founder, did something unexpected. He played that noise through a translation matrix of his own devising. This is a recording of what he heard.[...] Over time, Doctor Skarosa became convinced these were the voices of the recently departed. He believed it was a telepathic communication from the dead.'

---

[158] Jobs died three years earlier, on 5 October 2011.
[159] EVP as contact from the dead had previously been the premise of *White Noise* (2005), a horror film directed by *Doctor Who* (1996)'s director Geoffrey Sax.

All this is building up to a horrific revelation: the eerie voices, when decoded, turn out to be saying 'Don't cremate me!' – the 'three words' which 3W's name references. Chang elaborates:

> 'There is one simple, horrible possibility that has never occurred to anyone throughout human history. [...]The dead remain conscious. The dead are fully aware of everything that is happening to them.'[160]

This sustained effort to evoke a creeping horror in the viewer is, admittedly, one of the modes in which **Doctor Who** routinely operates – it can be seen in *Listen*, to name just one recent story. The subject matter, though, is particularly in keeping with the religious concepts underlying Samhain and All Hallows' Eve. A continuity with the certainties of conventional religion, which this horrific afterlife appears to confound, is even suggested by locating the 3W mortuary in St Paul's.

The transition from *Dark Water* to *Death in Heaven* brings a change of emphasis. While much of the material is equally horrific – converted corpses emerging from graves, poor Danny's living death – during the lengthy, pivotal graveyard scene a shift in viewpoint gradually becomes apparent. The two-parter has from the beginning been driven by remembrance of the dead, with Clara's intense grief for Danny leading to her desperate attempt to force the Doctor to undo his demise. Although his actual death, in a

---

[160] This is, of course, 3W's sales pitch, and there is little evidence of it in the story: what there is amounts to the sound file Chang plays, Danny's feeling of cold, and a scream which Seb attributes to someone having left their body to medical science.

routine road accident, is apparently random and meaningless – 'boring' and 'ordinary', as Clara tells her Gran – Danny has been defined throughout his appearances by his former military career, and his guilt at killing a civilian. His victim haunts him more literally than ever in the Nethersphere, present yet unspeaking like a more conventional, less technological ghost.

During *Death in Heaven*, the resurrected dead are increasingly typified by Danny himself. Indeed, with two exceptions (Dr Skarosa, who we never saw alive, and the Brigadier, who goes unrevealed until after the resolution of the main plot), there is no indication that any of the other Cybermen are anyone in particular. None of Missy's inductees from earlier in the season resurface; nor do the characters who die during the episode itself; nor anyone else of significance to Clara (such as her late mother or her own Victorian iteration). Even Danny's victim is never seen walking the world as a Cyberman. From around the 25- to the 45-minute mark of *Death in Heaven*, the episode's central narrative of the dead's return as soldiers in Missy's Cyber-army is personified in Danny.

The fact that Danny, and not the Brigadier, acts as the focus of this scene, fits perfectly with the popular British mythology of Remembrance Day, and of the First World War in particular, in which it is the bravery and self-sacrifice of the ordinary soldier which warrant the honour and admiration of posterity, rather than the wrong-headed generals and other senior officers whose whims so frequently cause their deaths. This view originates in the contemporary trench poetry of volunteers such as Siegfried Sassoon and Wilfred Owen, giving it the hallmark of first-person experience, and is expressed in such artefacts of popular culture as the film *Oh! What a Lovely War* (1969) and the sitcom **Blackadder**

95

Goes Forth (1989). It can be seen through science-fiction metaphor in **Doctor Who**'s own *The War Games*, in which the senior officers of the British and German armies in the trenches (as of the other historical conflicts which the War Lord has modelled in microcosm on his unnamed planet) are shown to be 'Aliens', using mind control and other forms of coercion to pit their troops against one another for their own spurious ends, when not chummily socialising together in their peaceful headquarters.

The resonance of this narrative, coupled with Danny's habitual division of the military into 'soldiers' and 'officers', overlaps uneasily with the Brigadier's presence in the story. In particular, the fact that Lethbridge-Stewart's Cyber-self pursues a personal agenda rather than contributing to Danny's big push, and thus lives to fight another day once all his enlisted comrades are dead, creates uncomfortable echoes of the First World War myth. This sits awkwardly with the Brigadier's established personality and the Doctor's admiration for him, but ties in perfectly with the democratising, anti-authoritarian view of the war – as, of course, does Danny's persistently expressed view of the officer class.

The tendency to forget, or worse deliberately to erase, this nuance, is a constant element in Remembrance Day celebrations in the UK. Far-right groups such as Britain First attempt to co-opt the iconography of the poppy to promote hatred [161]. Tabloid newspapers politicise the official wreath-laying ceremony at the Cenotaph in London, scrutinising the leaders of the political parties

---

[161] Foxton, Willard, 'The Loathsome Britain First Are Trying to Hijack The Poppy – Don't Let Them'.

for signs of insincerity[162]. Even the official charity, the Royal British Legion, has been accused of politicising and corporatising the annual event [163]. Critics perceive the mood as jingoistic and triumphalist.

Since 1934 a much smaller charity, the Peace Pledge Union, has distributed white poppies aimed at promoting an alternative, pacifist message of universal, rather than partisan, remembrance [164]. In Paul Cornell's Virgin **Doctor Who New Adventures** novel *Human Nature* (1995), from which *Human Nature / The Family of Blood* (2007) was adapted, Timothy Dean (the novel's equivalent of Tim Latimer) is a conscientious objector rather than a combatant during the Great War, assisting at the front lines as a Red Cross medic; and as an elderly man he and later the seventh Doctor wear one of these white poppies, rather than the red ones their counterparts and Martha wear in the televised story[165].

Cornell has called this alteration to the story's imagery 'mostly about the difference between a mainstream TV audience and a

---

[162] Greenslade, Roy, 'Rightwing Press Mounts Assault over Jeremy Corbyn's Cenotaph Nod'.
[163] Tweedy, Rod, 'My Name Is Legion – The British Legion and the Control of Remembrance'.
[164] 'White Poppy for a Culture of Peace'. The Peace Pledge Union has its origins in a coalition of anti-war movements, some of whose reasons for discouraging war with Nazi Germany were less than creditable. This does not reflect upon the sincerity of the present-day organisation.
[165] Cornell, Paul, *Human Nature* (1995), pp252-54.

97

niche fan one,'[166] implying perhaps that the former would find the anti-establishment message of the white poppy unpalatable. Nonetheless, the 2015 episode *The Zygon Inversion* (co-written by Moffat with Peter Harness[167]) places a similar message in the Doctor's mouth:

> 'When you fire that first shot, no matter how right you feel, you have no idea who's going to die! You don't know whose children are going to scream and burn – how many hearts will be broken – how many lives shattered – how much blood will spill until everybody does until what they were always going to have to do from the very beginning – sit down and talk!'

Moffat and Harness remind us that Doctor is no naïve pacifist, but has reached his position from first-hand experience of war:

> 'And do you know what you do with all that pain? Shall I tell you where you put it? You hold it tight till it burns your hand, and you say this: no one else will ever have to live like this. No one else will have to feel this pain. Not on my watch.'

Though Danny might not agree with the specifics of this, he and the Doctor have reached their positions through similarly traumatic experiences of war. Danny's sacrifice, and that of the Cyber-army he leads, is not a partisan gesture, nor one dedicated to the perpetuation of war: indeed, in ridding the Doctor of the army

---

[166] Cornell, Paul, Introduction to *Human Nature* (2015), pvi.
[167] The second half of a two-parter with *The Zygon Invasion*, written by Harness alone.

Missy seeks to encumber him with, it arguably spares the universe from such a fate. *The Zygon Inversion* – whose broadcast the day before Remembrance Sunday 2015 is perhaps the clearest indication of all that the themes and timing of *Death in Heaven* are not coincidental – must be seen as glossing and clarifying the Remembrance Day imagery of *Death in Heaven*, rejecting the narrow adoption of the red poppy as political propaganda to which the white poppies are a necessary counterweight.

It is essential to Danny's understanding of himself that he is an ordinary soldier, not an officer, and this places him perfectly to act as the Cyber-army's representative and spokesman. Whatever Missy's intentions in handing the Doctor this poisoned chalice, Danny is able to use it for good, an intention he expresses eloquently in his speech to his Cyber-comrades:

> 'This is not a good day. This is Earth's darkest hour – and look at you miserable lot. We are the fallen – but today, we shall rise. The army of the dead will save the land of the living. This is not the order of a general, nor the whim of a lunatic. [...] This is a promise. The promise of a soldier.'

'The Darkest Hour' was Winston Churchill's phrase for Britain's lone stand against the Nazis following the fall of France. (The wording has been foreshadowed by the Doctor's description of moments of destiny in *Dark Water*: 'This is it, Clara, one of those moments. [...] The darkest day. The blackest hour.') The more potent references here, though, are to the First World War. 'We are the fallen' echoes the rhetoric of two extremely well-known war poems, often read at Remembrance Day ceremonies: John McCrae's 'In Flanders

Fields'[168], which contains the line 'We are the Dead'; and Lawrence Binyon's 'For the Fallen'[169], from which the familiar lines beginning 'They shall not grow old, as we who are left grow old' come.

These references are allusive, rather than explicit. Neither Danny nor the Brigadier died in combat, and while all the dead of humanity are resurrected in *Death in Heaven*, there is nothing to remind us specifically that the victims of the two World Wars, and other wars, are among them. Nevertheless – and given all the caveats that this story lacks the dramatic space for, but which *The Zygon Inversion* later supplies – this speech offers the clearest statement of the relationship between the episodes' seasonal concerns. The tawdry clichés of Halloween are redeemed – hallowed, in fact – by Danny's act of remembrance, and the hordes of the risen undead become the army of the beloved fallen, by whose heroism the living are saved.

---

[168] First published in *Punch*, 8 December 1915.
[169] First published in *The Times*, 21 September 1914, and previously heard on **Doctor Who** in the final moments of *The Family of Blood*.

CHAPTER 4: 'QUEEN OF EVIL': TRANS-FIGURING THE MASTER

The motif of a mysterious woman on the periphery of the Doctor's life who knows things he does not, whose relationship with him is flirtatious as well as enigmatic, and who eventually becomes pivotal to major events in his life, is a staple of Steven Moffat's **Doctor Who** plotting. To varying extents (and on different timescales), Madame Kovarian, Clara, Ashildr/Me, Liz 10, Tasha Lem and the various incarnations of River Song all fit aspects of this profile[170]. The introduction of Missy in *Deep Breath*, nine episodes before she becomes a central character in *Dark Water*, clearly follows the pattern, and is remarkable primarily for the fact that she turns out – in keeping, for once, with the expectations of long-term fans regarding any character about whose identity there is some mystery – to be someone already known to the viewer[171].

---

[170] First introduced in *The Impossible Astronaut / Day of the Moon*, *Asylum of the Daleks*, *The Girl Who Died*, *The Beast Below*, *The Time of the Doctor* and *Silence in the Library / Forest of the Dead* respectively.

[171] Missy's intervening appearances mostly serve to reinforce her psychopompic role (*Into the Dalek*, *The Caretaker*) or to hint at her patronage of Clara (*Flatline*), but in *In the Forest of the Night*, her presence is more baffling. Here she professes surprise – and appears somewhat disappointed – when the Earth avoids destruction by a solar flare. Her interest in this, and how it would have related to her intentions for the Nethersphere and the Cybermen, are difficult to fathom, and the scene's function may be simply to remind the viewers of Missy's existence before her first meeting with the Doctor in the next episode. In any case, no

Brief though it is, Missy's first appearance includes a number of clues as to her true identity. She has (or affects to believe she has) a romantic history with the Doctor, referring to him as 'my boyfriend'. The relationship is one of influence, as she implies that her Scottish accent is adopted in imitation of his. She wears black period clothing, and acts in ways which could be seen as either childishly impulsive and uninhibited, or a performance of such behaviour (though the Half-Face Man is an unappreciative audience). All of this is consistent, either with long-term tendencies of the Master's character, or with the behaviour of the most recent incarnation played by John Simm, and it seems likely that a male character introduced in this way would have been swiftly identified by many viewers. The change of gender obscures the similarities enough for the revelation to surprise many of the audience, in the same way that the kindly alter ego taken on by the Derek Jacobi Master in *Utopia* (2007) helps to hide his identity until the opportune moment. In this respect, it serves an important dramatic function that should not be downplayed.

Nonetheless, the Master's gender-swap represents a significant departure for **Doctor Who**. Though science fiction (particularly as a literary genre) has used similar devices to explore the questions of sex and gender identity from a multiplicity of different angles, **Doctor Who** has on the whole been remarkably conservative on the issue. While Missy is not the first **Doctor Who** character to have ostensibly changed sex, such instances have been extremely

---

further clues to her identity are detectable until *Dark Water*, unless offering a guest tea in *Into the Dalek* counts.

few, given how many have belonged to species with advanced technologies and alien biologies; nor have these rare instances and their implications been explored in anything resembling depth.

Doctor Who has never been afraid of influence – to say the least – and science fiction would have offered a rich source of stories about gender to borrow from, had the scriptwriters been as interested in telling these as they were in stories about colonialism, capitalism or the futility of war[172]. True, to present any of these options during much of its history, **Doctor Who** would have had to negotiate some awkward boundaries regarding the presentation of sexuality in a 'family show', but these boundaries were becoming permeable by the late 1980s, and the 21st-century stories regularly feature characters in same-sex or interspecies relationships without exhibiting any such inhibitions.

The fact that Time Lords can change sex when they regenerate is now clearly established, but no Time Lord had previously been shown to have made this transition, despite 16 orthodox regenerations happening onscreen[173]. For the most part, **Doctor**

---

[172] See, for example, *The Mutants* (1972), *Colony in Space* (1971) and *The Silurians*. Works of literary SF whose scenarios involve mutable sex and gender include Ursula K le Guin's *The Left Hand of Darkness* (1969), Samuel R Delany's *Triton* (1976), and Iain M Banks's **Culture** novels, notably *The Player of Games* (1988).

[173] Up to this point the Doctor had regenerated 13 times onscreen, the Master once (*Utopia* – most of his other changes of body are not 'regenerations'), Romana once (*Destiny of the Daleks* (1979) – yes, we are counting that as once) and K'anpo once (*Planet of the Spiders*). Other characters have multiple bodies implying offscreen regenerations, notably Borusa and Rassilon. Non-Gallifreyans who

103

Who in the 20th and 21st centuries alike has depicted humanity's arrangement – of two complementary and fixed sexes, male and female, broadly resembling one another but with significant differences – as a universal expectation for sentient life, despite the fact that it is far from universal even amongst Earth's vertebrates. To the first approximation, only those populations whose members appear to be all male (like the Sensorites or Sontarans[174]) or all female (like the Drahvins or Cryons[175]) break this pattern of gender conformity. The vanishingly rare biological individuals who fail to obey this rule, such as the hermaphrodite Alpha Centaurian ambassador to Peladon, are referred to as 'he' anyway[176]. The assumption that a gender-indeterminate individual is male unless proven otherwise similarly affects the treatment of

---

regenerate using Time Lord methods are also seen to keep their previous sex (*Underworld* (1978), *Mawdryn Undead, Day of the Moon, Let's Kill Hitler*).

[174] *The Sensorites* (1964); *The Time Warrior* (1973-74) and multiple sequels. The Sontarans are explicitly all male: they are referred to as 'he', reproduce by cloning, and are confused by the very existence of female humans. Cases like the Sensorites – where we apparently see only males, and the question never comes up – are much more common.

[175] *Galaxy 4* (1965), *Attack of the Cybermen*. Again, this is explicit in the case of the Drahvins, and implicit in the case of the Cryons. Such species are much rarer in **Doctor Who**, despite the fact that Earth evolution has produced a number of all-female species but only a couple of dubious examples of all-male ones.

[176] *The Curse of Peladon* (1972), *The Monster of Peladon* (1974). Centauri is voiced by Ysanne Churchman, making the 'he' designation at least somewhat problematic for the viewer.

functionally neuter species such as Cybermen and Daleks: though we have seen women Cyber-converted [177] and are given no information about Dalek gender, the generic masculine is used, and individuals such as Handles and Rusty are 'he' by default[178].

Perhaps inevitably for a series such as **Doctor Who**, where the unfamiliar is often the monstrous and the monstrous is generally evil, most of the previous gender-swapping characters are villains like Missy. Kronos in *The Time Monster* (1972) is assumed to be male (though 'his' birdlike form has nothing especially masculine about it except its Corinthian helmet) until it manifests itself as a female face in episode 6; although Jo Grant is confused by this, the Chronovore makes it clear that it 'can be all things', and thus has no actual gender. A few shapeshifting characters are seen to inhabit bodies of more than one sex, but they were rarely convincingly gendered to begin with: Kamelion or Odda the Zygon may be labelled as 'he', again by default, but seeing them take the forms of Tegan or Sister Lamont creates little by way of gender confusion[179]. Had Lord Kiv survived for more than a short scene in Peri's body, that might have provided more scope for subverting the audience's expectations, but Nicola Bryant gets only two lines in the part before her new character is killed (in a scene which is later revealed to have been fabricated in any case)[180]. Dismissing all of these leaves us with only two sustained examples of gender-

---

[177] *The Age of Steel, Doomsday,* **Torchwood**: *Cyberwoman* (2006).
[178] *The Time of the Doctor, Into the Dalek.*
[179] *The King's Demons* (1983), *Terror of the Zygons* (1975).
[180] *The Trial of a Time Lord* episodes eight and 14.

swapping in prior **Doctor Who**: Eldrad in *The Hand of Fear* (1976) and Lady Cassandra in *New Earth* (2006).

As a silicon-based alien taking multiple forms, Eldrad runs the gamut of gender identities: initially a severed hand that survived a prehistoric spaceship crash, Eldrad is first an 'it' and then, once named, a 'he', before building a new body very loosely modelled on that of Sarah Jane Smith. Although this body appears more mineral than human, it is played (albeit with a deep voice and gender-neutral body-language) by Judith Paris, and is thus accorded female pronouns and even referred to by the Doctor as 'the lady'. Later, after she is apparently destroyed for a second time, Eldrad's 'true form' is restored, and proves to be a barely humanoid crystal played (with lumbering body-language and a positively booming voice) by serial monster actor Stephen Thorne. Sarah at once concludes that 'she' is now a 'he', and Eldrad uses the same pronoun to refer to another member of his species, apparently confirming Sarah's opinion (at least for **Doctor Who**'s default understanding of 'he'). Interestingly, the female Eldrad displays a more sympathetic personality than the male, persuading the Doctor and Sarah to return her to her homeworld and save her life, whereas her regenerated form is quickly revealed as a power-hungry megalomaniac and sent plummeting to his (presumably temporary) doom by the Doctor himself. Reflecting the writing of the two as essentially separate characters, Sarah's verdict could be an assessment of a couple after a dinner party: 'Well, I quite liked her, but I couldn't stand him.'

Lady Cassandra claims on her first appearance in *The End of the World* (2005) to have once been 'a little boy', but this has no obvious impact on the character depicted, being simply another surprising detail serving to alienate Rose from the far-future world. Given that Cassandra is hardly the most reliable of sources it may not even be true, and it is certainly undermined by her reaction in *New Earth* when, thanks to a literal plot device, she finds herself in the Doctor's body: 'Oh my, this is different. [...] Goodness me, I'm a man.' After she finds a final home in the body of her manservant Chip, her gratitude to him and her acceptance that her new body is failing lead to a time-bending reconciliation in which a younger Cassandra – for the first time played by Zoe Wanamaker in person, rather than appearing as a special effect – comforts her dying future self, who Sean Gallagher as Chip plays with a convincing imitation of her vocal and bodily mannerisms[181].

Both of these are clear examples of a character being played first by an actor of one sex and then of another; both raise questions of language and gender expression, and give these actors an opportunity to act, and the other actors and the audience an opportunity to respond, outside the conventional codes for the presentation of gender to which **Doctor Who** – and indeed most television – habitually adheres. Cassandra's identification with her host bodies retains a self-aware distance, however, expressed in terms of aesthetic judgements, while Eldrad is essentially a rock sculpted into different shapes. Neither is what the reinvention of the Master as Missy represents: a character who is at one time a

---

[181] Certainly more so than David Tennant's.

man and another a woman, these gender identities overlaying and inflecting the fundamental personality which underlies them[182].

At first glance – and indeed, on deeper inspection – Steven Moffat might seem an unlikely candidate for the first **Doctor Who** scriptwriter to explore such a transformation. Much of his writing output betrays a gender essentialism which is at odds with the feminist understanding of gender as a social construct. It repeatedly assumes that particular characteristics are innate to each sex – a view that may not be inherently misogynistic (as it sees both sexes as flawed, and assigns women some superior qualities, such as an ability to transcend their sex drives), but can certainly be called sexist.

---

[182] Some definitions follow for readers who may, like the author, be less well-versed in gender theory than they might like. **Gender identity** refers to a person's internal sense of placement on the gender spectrum (as a man, a woman or another kind of person); it is not the same as **sex** (a biological property of a person's body, which may be male, female or intersex), **gender expression** (the gendered ways a person acts, which may be masculine, feminine or something other) or **sexual orientation** (which relates purely to the types of people to whom someone is attracted). **Gender dysphoria** can be experienced when one's gender identity does not align with one's biological sex. **Transgender** – often abbreviated to **trans** – describes people whose gender identity differs from that assigned to them at birth. A **trans woman** was assigned a male identity at birth but identifies as female; a **trans man** vice versa. **Transsexual** is a less popular term referring to those who make a physical transition between sexes. **Misgendering** means referring to someone in a way which is inappropriate to their gender identity. **Genderfluid** describes people whose gender identity varies with time.

108

The humour in a typical episode of Moffat's sitcom **Coupling** (2000-04) rests on such unexamined assumptions about what men and women are like. His and Mark Gatiss' **Sherlock** (2010-) contrasts with its US rival **Elementary** (2012-) in its unwillingness to reinvent characters across gender boundaries[183]. At least two of his **Doctor Who** stories are egregiously sexist, with the Doctor in 2011 twice ascribing River Song's disruptive effect on his life to the fact that she is 'a woman'[184]. The same year's uncharacteristically mystical Christmas special, *The Doctor, the Widow and the Wardrobe*, softens this by portraying women – by virtue of their ability to become mothers – as stronger than men, suggesting that this is part of 'the base code of nature itself'. While ostensibly more respectful to (fertile) women, this again evinces an essentialist philosophy of gender.

At the same time, Moffat's stories have been more open than those of his predecessors to the always controversial idea that the Doctor might be played by a female actor. Dialogue written by him for *The End of Time* clarifies that male Time Lords can become women when they regenerate[185], and his 'The Night of the Doctor'

---

[183] **Elementary** features Lucy Liu as Dr Watson, Natalie Dormer as Moriarty and transsexual actor Candis Cayne as Mrs Hudson; the equivalent parts in **Sherlock** are played by Martin Freeman, Andrew Scott and Una Stubbs. (Although Moffat's **Doctor Who** takes the altogether more progressive view that Conan Doyle's original Holmes stories were written about a lesbian dinosaur.)
[184] *Let's Kill Hitler, The Wedding of River Song.*
[185] 'I'm a girl! No. No, I'm not a girl.' (*The End of Time* episode 2). Davies confirms in *The Writer's Tale* that Moffat wrote the 11th Doctor's introductory dialogue (p654).

confirms that the Sisterhood of Karn, at least, can induce such a change. In Neil Gaiman's *The Doctor's Wife* (2011) the Doctor reminisces about his Time Lord friend the Corsair, who was male and female at different times[186] (although he finds this unusual enough to warrant slightly ribald comment): and while Gaiman reports that Moffat made other changes to the Corsair's history[187], he evidently did not veto the character's gender-switching propensities. A year after *Death in Heaven*, Moffat's *Hell Bent* would become the first story to portray a gender-switching regeneration unambiguously onscreen[188]. And in *Death in Heaven* itself, after Missy has been positively confirmed as a female incarnation of the Master, Moffat plays with the idea of a female Doctor both metafictionally in the opening credits, and in the later idea that the Doctor might become queen of Gallifrey[189].

---

[186] The implication is that the Corsair changed gender more than once. Gaiman's short story 'Eleven Things You Probably Didn't Know About the Corsair' depicts the fourth Corsair as male, the fifth and seventh female, and the eighth and ninth male (Hickman, Clayton, ed, *The Brilliant Book 2012*, p63).
[187] Gaiman, Neil, 'A Fairly Humongous **Doctor Who** Q&A Mostly'.
[188] The General – played by Ken Bones in *The Day of the Doctor*, *The Time of the Doctor* (in voiceover) and *Hell Bent* – regenerates after being shot by the Doctor, into an incarnation played by T'Nia Miller. She states that the Bones incarnation was 'the only time I've been a man', meaning she has changed gender twice. (This regeneration also changes the General's apparent ethnicity from white to black, resolving another tedious fan controversy.)
[189] See also *The Magician's Apprentice*:
CLARA
Since when do you care about the Doctor?

110

Indeed, more than a decade before he became **Doctor Who**'s showrunner, Moffat was responsible for the only female Doctor to appear in a BBC broadcast to date, albeit in a story generally dismissed as a 'parody skit'. Although his time in charge of **Doctor Who** proper has been mercifully free of one-liners about farting and slug bestiality, a viewing of the 23-minute Comic Relief **Doctor Who** sketch *The Curse of Fatal Death* (1999) casts an intriguing light on the material Moffat has included. This ranges from predestination paradoxes to jokes about the Daleks' uses for chairs; even the line 'Look after the universe for me – I've put a lot of work into it' resurfaces intact in the 'Prologue' to the 2015 season. Most significantly for our current purposes, this Doctor's final regeneration into Joanna Lumley leads to a blossoming romance between her and Jonathan Pryce's Master, as well as jokes about breasts[190].

From the point of view of inclusivity this might be seen as a backward step, in that in *The Curse of Fatal Death* as in *Death in*

MISSY

Since always. Since the Cloister Wars. Since the night he stole the moon and the President's wife. Since he was a little girl. One of those was a lie. Can you guess which one?

Hell Bent revisits the first two of these, but is ultimately ambiguous about how far they can be considered true.

[190] That Moffat is not above playing the idea of gender transition for laughs is confirmed in the final episode of **Coupling**, *Nine and a Half Months* (2004), in which the perennially sex-starved Jeff returns in a dream sequence as 'Jeffina', having taken his obsession with the female body to its logical conclusion.

111

Heaven it takes a change of sex to bring what was formerly a same-sex attraction out into the open. (*The Curse of Fatal Death* takes this heteronormative approach even further, as the change also induces the Doctor's fiancée Emma to leave her on the grounds that 'You're just not the man I fell in love with.') What it does show, though, is how Moffat's clear interest in issues of gender identity can combine with SF tropes of sudden gender reassignment, to explore the more progressive question of what actual alterations to a person's core identity and character – and their treatment by others – such a change might bring.

Unlike Jo and Sarah when confronted by the re-gendered Kronos and Eldrad, nobody in *Dark Water / Death in Heaven* expresses puzzlement at the Master's new sex. In this respect, the characters have the advantage over the audience, some of whom may struggle to accept that Michelle Gomez's character is the same as was played in the past by Roger Delgado, Anthony Ainley et al. An androgynous performance like Judith Paris's Eldrad would doubtless have been more palatable to some, but although otherwise the character evinces considerable continuity with her earlier incarnations, there is no ambiguity in Missy's gender expression. She wears dresses, kisses the Doctor, claims to be the 'Queen of Evil', calls her promise to kill Osgood 'our secret girl plan', refers to the Cybermen as 'my boys' and herself as their 'Mummy', and uses uncharacteristic birth imagery[191]. Viewers who are resistant to this based on their own preconceptions about

---

[191] 'All the graves of the planet Earth are about to give birth' [*Dark Water*].

112

gender identity will find the character's presentation accords them little sympathy.

Certainly the Doctor, though initially appalled at discovering the Master is still alive, seems unfazed by her transition. He consistently refers to Missy as 'she', and avoids male pronouns even when recalling their childhood:

> 'I had a friend once. We ran together when I was little, and I thought we were the same. When we grew up, we weren't. Now she's trying to tear the world apart, and I can't run fast enough to hold it together.'

The other characters' reactions vary. Osgood's is the most confused response: she takes the change of pronoun seriously, even referring retrospectively to the Simm Master as 'she' ('We do have files on all our ex-prime ministers. She wasn't even the worst.'), but is also the only person to use the title 'Master' after Missy renounces it[192]. The first time is when she correctly guesses the character's past identity – the story's only reference to the regeneration, other than Missy's initial revelation – and the second in understandable panic after Missy threatens to kill her. (Since this is this Osgood's final line, it may even be that this misgendering is what persuades Missy to follow through with the threat.)

The response of the Cyber-converted Brigadier would be worth understanding, since other than the Doctor he is as far as we know

---

[192] This continues to apply in *The Magician's Apprentice* / *The Witch's Familiar*, where the character's former name goes unmentioned (although Ashildr uses it in her absence in *Hell Bent*).

the story's only character to have met the Master as a man...[193] but as he has no dialogue or facial expression and minimal body language, all we can say is that he shows none of the compunction we might expect in killing a woman (even if she has just tried to kill his daughter). Quite what this might imply about his attitude to the change is impossible to say.

The other characters treat Missy as the woman – specifically, the female villain – she now is. Overall, the transition from the Master to Missy is, from the point of view of the characters and the programme, remarkably smooth and matter-of-fact, and the new status quo once established goes more or less unquestioned.

Moffat has been praised for his handling of this by transgender viewers:

> 'I'm pleasantly surprised. The parallels to transgender experience were handled with more grace than most media that is explicitly about trans people. The Doctor avoids misgendering her, even when talking about the past. The Mistress is every bit the over-the-top scheming villain she's always been; they don't tone down anything, they don't make her feel like a different character. She follows logically from John Simm's performance.'
>
> [Anna Wiggins, 'Regeneration: A Personal History of **Doctor Who**']

---

[193] Although most of them presumably remember Harold Saxon as prime minister as Osgood does. (They will also have temporarily turned into him, but it is ambiguous whether the characters in *The End of Time* remember this.)

114

'What is useful, and helpful to the trans community is how well her pronouns and name are handled after we find out who she is. [...] The way this was followed up with the Doctor's quiet acceptance that he may [...] one day experience a cross-gender regeneration himself is the icing on the cake [...]This is the sort of thing that does wonders for acceptance.'

[Michelle Kerry, 'Little Boxes Will Make You Angry: **Doctor Who** and Transphobia']

Kerry in particular contrasts Moffat's approach with Davies's, suggesting that the vain, surgery-obsessed Cassandra can be read as an 'offensive stereotype' of transgender women – although she acknowledges that equating femaleness with motherhood in *The Doctor, the Widow and the Wardrobe* is also less than friendly to trans people[194].

Where Kerry and Wiggins differ is in whether Missy should be read as a 'transgender' character in the real-world sense. Kerry rejects the idea that Time Lords are likely to experience gender dysphoria (arguing that if they did they would voluntarily regenerate until their sex changed) and instead considers them 'an analogue for genderfluid people'. Wiggins, on the other hand, argues for a reading where the Master 'has always been a woman. She has secretly hoped, in the deepest part of her mind that she seldom even allows herself to look at, for a feminine body, every time she regenerated'. Wiggins' argument, while heartfelt, relies on guesses about the state of mind of a character whose inner thoughts we

---

[194] Her criticism of Toby Whithouse is considerably stronger.

115

are almost never given access to[195]. While television has techniques available to indicate a character's inner life – voiceovers, dream and fantasy sequences, point-of-view shots – these have rarely been applied to the Master, in previous stories or here, and never in ways that particularly suggest gender identity. In their absence, we have only visible words and actions to judge by, and prior to Gomez's appearance the Master's have always conformed to our masculine expectations.

The experience of transgender people may indeed be the nearest real-world analogue to Missy's transformation, and Kerry and Wiggins demonstrate the value of reading it as a metaphor for such an experience. It is the nature of metaphors, however, that they are not literally the thing they signify, and in science fiction and fantasy in particular, human experiences can be signified by elements and imagery alien to human experience.

To what extent, then, is Gomez's Missy merely the same old Master in a new body, like the Simm or Jacobi incarnations; and to what extent is she, like the male Eldrad, a new character notionally continuing the history of the old?

Writing for the fanzine *Matrix* some 18 years before *Dark Water* was broadcast, the **Doctor Who** novelist and critic Daniel O'Mahony offered a penetrating critique of the Master, who he

---

[195] It is, at least, too subjective a reading to inform **Black Archive** editorial policy, which is to use 'the Master' (and 'he') for all appearances up to *The End of Time*, and 'Missy' (and 'she') from *Deep Breath* onwards.

116

described as 'the series' all-time worst villain'[196]. The Master was, he wrote, a plot function rather than a character; a Moriarty who was never permitted (except once, in *Logopolis* (1981)) to kill his Holmes, and was thus relegated from the role of 'nemesis' to that of 'archenemy'; a formulaic prop created during the most formulaic era of a series which is at its best when it eschews formula entirely. A particular complaint was that the Master's perennial conflict with the Doctor was rarely justified by anything beyond the expected enmity between the two, with the 1980s in particular seeing the character crop up repeatedly without pretext and generally with the flimsiest of aims.

> 'For the Doctor and the Master to clash time and time again suggests that the Master must be actively seeking our hero out [...] and Anthony Ainley's turn in the role just doesn't conjure the malignant hatred for his old enemy that such an approach would require. [...] What does the Master want the Xeraphin for[197]? Why does he plan to wreck Magna Carta[198]? What are his aims in 19th-century England[199]? These things are never properly rationalised [...]'[200]

---

[196] O'Mahony, Daniel, 'We Meet Again, Doctor...'. *Licence Denied* does not date the articles it reprints, but O'Mahony refers to *Doctor Who* (1996), broadcast and released on VHS in May 1996, and *Licence Denied* was published in November 1997.
[197] *Time-Flight.*
[198] *The King's Demons.*
[199] *The Mark of the Rani* (1985).
[200] O'Mahony p131.

O'Mahony's assessment is brutal but thoughtful, and warrants a full reading. Certainly successive **Doctor Who** scriptwriters, script editors and showrunners have had trouble working out what to do with the Master. He has been reinvented repeatedly, and more comprehensively than the Doctor himself. Sometimes such reinventions are effective: *The Deadly Assassin* (1976) makes him a decayed vampire, leeching the arcane energies of the Time Lords; the trilogy from *The Keeper of Traken* (1981) to *Castrovalva* (1982), a Miltonic Satan bringing entropic corruption to the universe; *Survival*, a Kurtz from Conrad's *Heart of Darkness*, a civilised man fascinated by and ultimately embracing the savagery surrounding him. For every such imaginative treatment, however, there are others where he is a leering, cackling pantomime villain, and the best the audience can hope for is that the stereotype is played (as it is by Eric Roberts in *Doctor Who* (1996)) entertainingly and with self-awareness.

The character's 21st-century reintroduction in *Utopia* begins with a similar reimagining, as we see in the transformed Professor Yana what the Master could have been like without his urge to evil: a flawed but noble-minded and supremely gifted scientist, wearily doing his best to save the vestiges of the human race; a man, indeed, much like some iterations of the Doctor himself. When Jacobi's performance turns, at the opening of a pocket-watch, to resurgent villainy, he amply displays the 'malignant hatred' O'Mahony found wanting in Ainley's interpretation. Yet – while the revelation of the Professor's true identity is effectively horrifying because we know the Master is evil – we are no closer to knowing **why** he is evil, when his alter ego Yana was not.

Simm's 'turn in the role', from the ending of *Utopia* to *The End of Time*, largely forgoes that overt malevolence in favour of a vicious schoolboy mockery, tinged with the somewhat camp self-awareness of the Roberts incarnation[201]. In explaining his villainy, however, Russell T Davies – who has been successful elsewhere when reinventing **Doctor Who** archetypes as convincing characters – disappoints. The reason given is a convoluted science-fiction device with no analogue in the real world: the Master has been driven insane by an incessant rhythm in his head, implanted retroactively in his childhood by the supreme Time Lord Rassilon, to act as a homing beacon, to restore Gallifrey from the time lock imposed by the Time War[202]. As character motivations go, this fails even to achieve the level of psychobabble, instead falling back into technobabble. Effectively, the character still has no reason for his villainy beyond the formulaic demand for an archenemy.

Davies's Master stories do introduce a new character element, however – or at least make explicit one which was previously at most a subtext. Unlike Holmes and Moriarty, the Doctor and the Master were once friends, a fact which is first mentioned explicitly in *The Sea Devils* (1972)[203] but which explains the mutual respect

---

[201] For simplicity's sake, we will be assuming that each actor to play the Master represents an 'incarnation', while acknowledging that this is inaccurate within the fiction.

[202] *The Sound of Drums*, *The End of Time* episode 2.

[203] 'Well, he used to be a friend of mine once. A very good friend. In fact, you might almost say we were at school together.' This is corroborated in *The Time Monster* and *The Five Doctors*, and *The Sound of Drums* makes it clear that they knew one another as children.

119

visible in Pertwee's and Delgado's performances. The regard between the characters during this period is expressed in a restrained, sardonic way, but a greater depth of feeling is implied when we learn that one of the Master's greatest fears is of the Doctor laughing at him[204].

Davies's scripts emphasise this friendship between the two men, while summarily dismissing the possibility (raised by some readings of a dubious line in *Planet of Fire* (1984)[205]) that they might be brothers[206]. He moves the Master's obsession with the Doctor into the realm of open flirtation, with lines like 'I like when you use my name,' 'Are you asking me out on a date?'[207] and 'Dying in your arms. Happy now?'[208]

Davies was not the first **Doctor Who** fan to detect a hint of sublimated sexuality in the Time Lords' rivalry, nor were his stories the first to portray the Master with gay undertones: the

---

[204] *The Mind of Evil* (1971). This is a rare occasion when we are indeed made privy to the Master's inner life

[205] The line is not easy to make out, but seems to be 'Won't you show mercy to your own – ?' It could be complete in itself, but the story's director Fiona Cumming reports that producer John Nathan-Turner believed it would have ended 'brother' (*Planet of Fire* DVD commentary).

[206] *The Sound of Drums*:

MARTHA
I thought you were going to say he was your secret brother or something.

DOCTOR
You've been watching too much TV.

[207] *The Sound of Drums*.

[208] *Last of the Time Lords*.

flamboyantly-dressed Roberts Master kisses Chang Lee as well as Grace[209], while the Ainley incarnation spends much of his final episode leading a leather-clad young man around on a leash[210]. Davies was, however, the first writer on the TV show proper to raise the issue of the Master's sexuality openly, rather than implicitly[211].

The first line of the Master's Michelle Gomez incarnation, immediately following her introduction of herself as 'Missy', refers to the Doctor as 'my boyfriend'[212], although the natural (and correct) assumption is that she is delusional on this point. Moffat's version of the Master has yet to mention the drumbeat which so plagued her Jacobi and Simm incarnations (and, implicitly, Delgado, Ainley, Roberts and the rest), leaving open the question of whether it has been exorcised. Instead, she has begun, almost unprecedentedly, to act in ways which, while vicious and immoral, are rooted in recognisable motivations. In *Dark Water / Death in Heaven*, Missy wants to prove to the Doctor that his moral superiority is just an affectation, so that the two of them can be friends again. In *The Magician's Apprentice / The Witch's Familiar*, she actually hopes to save him from death at Davros's hand.

---

[209] *Doctor Who* (1996).
[210] *Survival*.
[211] A contemporary commentary from Moffat on Davies's characterisation comes in 'Time Crash', where the Doctor jokingly refers to Lucy Saxon as the Master's 'beard' (a term used for the wife of a gay man, acquired to disguise his homosexuality).
[212] *Deep Breath*.

121

Unlike Clara, who is seen throughout 2014 to be becoming progressively more like the Doctor, Missy consistently wants the Doctor to become more like her. In *Hell Bent* Ashildr calls her 'The lover of chaos... who wants you to love it too', and the thrust of that season's 'Hybrid Prophecy' arc story is that Missy has brought the Doctor and Clara together to create a force of chaos that will destroy Gallifrey[213]. The ways she goes about achieving these aims are elaborate, convoluted and at times absurd – she is, after all, the Master still – but we finally understand what drives her to them: why, in fact, 'the Master must be actively seeking our hero out'. Put simply, she is in love with the Doctor, and always has been.

While his apparent motivelessness may be an impediment to describing him as a character rather than a plot device – and while his personality changes, like the Doctor's, in sometimes dramatic ways – the Master in his male incarnations has nevertheless had some consistent traits, some tendencies that increase with time and some recurring character points, which Missy continues to demonstrate in *Dark Water / Death in Heaven*. Some of these, like her penchants for grandiose scheming and casual yet sadistic killing, are standard villainous calling-cards, but others she shares with the Doctor himself. Her arrogance and sense of humour closely match his, for instance, particularly in his 12th incarnation:

---

[213] Her attempt in *The Witch's Familiar* to manipulate him into killing Clara seems at the time to run counter to her original matchmaking, but looks in retrospect like an opportunistic attempt to provoke the reaction later prompted naturally by the events of *Face the Raven*.

'Human beings are born dying. Your lifespans are hilarious.'

[Missy, *Death in Heaven*]

'Have you seen the size of human brains? They're hilarious.'

[The Doctor, *Listen*]

The difference here is that Missy is cruelly taunting Osgood before killing her, whereas the Doctor is (probably) just thoughtless in making light of Clara's human limitations. Nevertheless, the similar phrasing and sentiment are telling.

Missy's appreciation of Earth's popular culture (in her appropriation of Toni Basil's 1982 single 'Mickey', her comment that 'I love the telly here' and her Mary Poppins cosplay[214]) echoes the eclectic tastes of the Delgado and Simm Masters, seen to enjoy both pop music[215] and children's television[216]. The methodology of Gomez's plan is equally reminiscent of these incarnations:

---

[214] *Death in Heaven*, *The Magician's Apprentice*. 'Mickey' is a cover version of a 1979 song, 'Kitty' by Racey, although the lines Missy adapts are not in the original. Interestingly, Basil's version swaps the genders of the song's narrator and addressee, which involves her singing the line 'Any way you want to do it, I'll take it like a man.'

[215] King Crimson, Rogue Traders and Scissor Sisters, in *The Mind of Evil*, *The Sound of Drums* and *Last of the Time Lords* respectively.

[216] **The Clangers** (1969-72, 2015-) and **Teletubbies** (1997-2001, 2015-), in *The Sea Devils* and *The Sound of Drums* respectively. Missy is shown in *The Magician's Apprentice* to be a fan of **Play School** (1964-88).

weaponising alien species against humans was a speciality of her Delgado persona [217], but the Simm incarnation honed the technique, twice planning as Gomez does here to turn the entire human population into members of another species serving at his command [218].

Though Missy's association with death as guardian and psychopomp of the Nethersphere is a novel one, her predecessors were presented on various occasions as symbolic of death – skull-faced, body-snatching and antithetical to life [219]. As Gomez takes control of an army of animated skeletons (telling the Doctor that she is 'the one you left for dead' [220]), the commonality becomes more apparent. When describing death, her language is powerfully evocative: 'Human beings are born dying [...] You know, from the minute you slop out – you're rotting, decaying. The stench of you...'

Missy's behaviour and language are also in keeping with the general presentation of the Master as insane, though her self-identification as 'bananas' suggests an exceptional awareness of the fact [221]. Madness is a difficult trait to quantify in reality, but rather less so in popular drama and fiction, where the conventions

---

[217] This is true of every Delgado story except *Colony in Space*, though it is a single alien as often as an army.

[218] The Toclafane in *The Sound of Drums / Last of the Time Lords*, 'the Master race' in *The End of Time*, Cybermen in *Dark Water / Death in Heaven*.

[219] *The Deadly Assassin*, *The Keeper of Traken* and *The End of Time*.

[220] *Dark Water*.

[221] *Death in Heaven*. Simm is at least aware that others see him this way: 'All these years, you thought I was mad' [*The End of Time* episode 1].

124

for depicting it rarely match the distressing realities of real-world mental illness, and are incidentally often inflected by gender. Of the 20th-century Masters, Delgado appeared tightly controlled, though prone to occasional explosive outbursts of anger, but his successors were more overtly megalomaniacal, often displaying the seething hatred and gloating malice which (we might assume) the Delgado incarnation was repressing all along. Such a power-hungry urge for dominance is generally depicted as a masculine form of insanity, and from *The Deadly Assassin* onwards, the Master is repeatedly referred to as 'mad' or 'insane'.

The Simm incarnation's insanity – also noted frequently by those who encounter him – takes a different form. Though his egotism is intact (as the statues of him which litter *Last of the Time Lords*'s subjugated Earth attest), he is also childish, mercurial and lacking in impulse control, characteristics which were not typical of his past selves (including, from what little we see of him, Jacobi). Gomez is calmer than Simm, but in other ways her erratic unpredictability, inappropriate intimacies, frequent non-sequiturs and mayfly attention span are exaggerations of his behaviour. These fit an influential modern dramatic stereotype of specifically female madness, particularly common in the works of Joss Whedon and Neil Gaiman: among others, Drusilla in **Buffy the Vampire Slayer**, River Tam in **Firefly** (2002), Delirium in the **Sandman** comics (1989-96) and 'Idris' in *The Doctor's Wife* all fit the mould[222]. (Rather uncomfortably, this paradigm is not dissimilar from the so-called

---

[222] The portrayal of Andrew Scott's Moriarty in **Sherlock** is similar, though more overtly malevolent. Significantly, the character is also coded as gay.

125

'Manic Pixie Dream Girl' archetype, a model of female desirability in modern media[223].)

This differential gendering of madness raises a further question, which is that of the Master's attitude to women – and it is here, if anywhere, that the idea of the Master as a trans woman suffering from gender dysphoria falls down. As we have seen, Missy exhibits no ambiguity in her gender expression, but revels in her womanhood. Yet her predecessors seem to identify just as strongly as male – just as their explosive megalomania fits the masculine stereotype of villainous madness.

The character's 20th-century incarnations show a patronising surface gallantry which is unremarkable among **Doctor Who** villains of their era (and indeed characterises the earlier incarnations of the Doctor himself), but Davies brings out the inherent sexism of this, making his Master a misogynist. On being shot by Chantho, Jacobi's response is telling: 'Killed by an insect… a girl. How inappropriate.'[224] The Simm Master's wife, Lucy Saxon, is clearly subservient to him in *The Sound of Drums*, and her bruised face and flat affect in *Last of the Time Lords* suggest an abusive relationship in which she is not the abuser. She, too, ultimately shoots him, prompting a similar response: 'Always the women.'

This suggests that the male Masters appreciate their status as men as much as Gomez's Missy does hers as a woman. Her choice of terminology emphasises the distinction: in place of the originally

---

[223] 'Manic Pixie Dream Girl', TV Tropes.
[224] *Utopia*.

patriarchal, but now gender-neutral[225], terms 'Time Lord' and 'Master', she opts for the feminised 'Time Lady' and 'Mistress', claiming to be 'old-fashioned'[226]. Unlikely as it seems that a species biologically capable of gender-swapping would espouse a sexist ideology at all, it is the more implausible that a character with such a view of language **and** gender dysphoria would have opted for the title 'Master' in the first place. At best, we would have to assume a character in deep denial, seething with jealous resentment against those who were lucky enough to have female bodies matching their gender identities – a description it is difficult to square with many of Gomez's predecessors.

A neater solution to the conundrum lies in a personality trait, not of the Master's but of the Doctor's: he is, to all appearances, a man of the heterosexual persuasion. First introduced to us as a grandfather[227], he associates with a long succession of attractive young women[228], and while his first seven incarnations were largely chaste, *Doctor Who* (1996) gave the Master every opportunity to

---

[225] Other than Susan, who never uses the term, the series' most prominent female Time Lord is Romana. She calls herself 'a Time Lord' in *The Pirate Planet* (1978) and *The Creature from the Pit* (1979), and never self-identifies as a 'Time Lady' (though the Doctor (*City of Death* (1979)) and Adric (*State of Decay* (1980)) apply the term to her, in its only uses onscreen prior to *Dark Water*). The title 'Master' is widely used in academia regardless of gender.
[226] *Dark Water*, and later *The Witch's Familiar*.
[227] 'An Unearthly Child'.
[228] Attractive young men are a great deal rarer, though the second Doctor and Jamie in particular seem close.

observe his susceptibility to the charms of blonde American surgeons. Since then, the Doctor has been portrayed as in love with Rose (his duplicate even settling down with her when given the opportunity), and has been married three times to our knowledge, to Marilyn Monroe, Elizabeth I and River Song[229]. True, he accepts (but does not initiate) a brief kiss from Captain Jack, and offers to care for the dying Simm Master[230], but it is a large stretch to imagine such a man entering a same-sex relationship.

Of those Earth organisms that change gender naturally – 'sequential hermaphrodites' – the most common vertebrates are those species of fish who are able change sex during their lifecycle, and normally do so in response to reproductive pressures – just as the Master's change of sex to complement the Doctor's occurs once they are apparently the only remaining pair of Time Lords in the universe. Whether it is prompted by this kind or biological imperative or not, Missy's latest regeneration – 'the upgrade', as she will later refer to it[231] – removes this barrier to the fulfilment of her desires.

(A point of comparison which was not available during *Dark Water / Death in Heaven* is the behaviour of, and her subordinate Gastron's reaction to, the regenerated General in *Hell Bent*. Gastron is clearly surprised that his superior has changed gender, looking disconcerted before correcting his initial 'Are you all right, sir?' with an 'I'm sorry – ma'am.' This suggests that gender-

---

[229] *A Christmas Carol, The Day of the Doctor, The Wedding of River Song.*
[230] *The Parting of the Ways, Last of the Time Lords.*
[231] *The Witch's Familiar.*

swapping regenerations are not routine, even on Gallifrey[232]. The new General feels that she is 'back to normal', and observes of her experience as a man, 'How do you cope with all that ego'? Though we might put this down to – again unlikely – sexist assumptions on the General's part, the implication is that what Moffat believes to be the inherent characteristics of men and women are superimposed over the fundamental personal qualities of regenerating Time Lords. However, her behaviour is not in fact much altered, and her brusquely military persona retains elements of conventional masculinity that Missy clearly does not.)

A final observation about the Master's character completes the picture: when overtaken by changes he cannot control, he opts to revel in them, throwing himself wholeheartedly into his changed identity. This can be seen in his bestial response to the Cheetah contagion in *Survival*, his reckless willingness to burn up his bodily energies when restored to unstable life in *The End of Time*, and even his adoption of Americanisms when possessing the body of Bruce in *Doctor Who* (1996)[233].

By this interpretation, the Master was never sexist by conviction: rather, his sexism has been opportunistic. Finding himself in a male body in a patriarchal society, he has accepted and ruthlessly

---

[232] It also confirms that Gallifreyan language uses gendered terminology – odd though this might seem – and thus that the 'Master'/'Mistress' and 'Lord'/'Lady' distinctions are not just Missy entertaining herself with the peculiarities of English.

[233] Admittedly his reaction to being shrunk to action-figure size in *Planet of Fire* is less positive, but this is a change which, as the story shows, he stands a realistic chance of reversing.

paraded the advantages his gender afforded him, including the opportunity to gratify his sadism by beating his wife. Equally, finding herself a woman in a culture where feminism, sisterhood and 'girl power' are, while not dominant, at least present as cultural phenomena, she embraces her female identity and makes as much of it as she possibly can.

There is an element of performance to all these responses, as there is to everything the character does: they are done for the benefit of an audience. In reality this audience is of course us, but within the fiction it is always the Doctor. Now she has the opportunity, Missy will play his girlfriend with all the conviction she can muster. Now one of the great barriers to their romance has been, in her view, eliminated, the first baroque and labyrinthine scheme of this incarnation is aimed at removing the other – his high-minded distaste for her moral choices, which she is determined to prove to him are so much hot air.

To Missy, the Doctor's willingness to kill her in *Death in Heaven* is the most positive signal he can have sent her in ages. In accompanying it with the words 'You win', he is practically leading her on.

CHAPTER 5. 'HOW MAY I ASSIST YOU WITH YOUR DEATH?': DEATH AND WHAT COMES AFTER

For a series whose stock-in-trade is violent death[234], **Doctor Who** is generally reluctant to explore its effects on those left behind. Bereavement is shown frequently, in the sense that we see a character die to whom another is related, romantically attached or otherwise close, but its consequences are usually confined to the immediate trauma (often because the bereaved are motivated towards short-term self-sacrifice as a result).

For the regular characters, such trauma is often visible, but there is little acknowledgement of long-term emotional impact. Companions in 20th-century **Doctor Who** are not infrequently recent orphans or lone survivors of massacres, but all of them – even Nyssa, who outlives not only her father and stepmother but her civilisation, her species and a large proportion of the neighbouring cosmos [235] – demonstrate remarkable emotional resilience. On the very rare occasions when the dead include a regular character – the most significant example being Nyssa's contemporary Adric[236] – their passing is marked at the time by

---

[234] The 'Time Team' feature in DWM #490 reported the cumulative count of onscreen deaths in **Doctor Who** up to and including *The End of Time* as 1,899, an average of around 9.5 deaths per story.
[235] In *The Keeper of Traken* and *Logopolis*.
[236] Katarina ('The Traitors', *The Daleks' Master Plan* episode 4, 1965), Kamelion (*Planet of Fire*) and Sara Kingdom ('Destruction of Time', *The Daleks' Master Plan* episode 12, 1966) are killed after

solemnity, then swiftly dismissed as a distraction from the matter in hand. They receive no funeral rites, their bodies tending to be conveniently pulverised, exploded or sucked out into space.

This is of course routine for an action-adventure series: no protagonist whose adventures brought them so habitually into contact with death could function if each passing left them paralysed with grief. *Black Orchid* (1982), a uniquely domestic and personal story for 20th-century **Doctor Who**, demonstrates its eccentricity by having the Doctor actually attend the funeral of the story's tragic, insane antagonist George Cranleigh – something he had apparently never thought to do in nearly 20 years of televised adventures, and rarely has since. The only prominent funerals in the 21st-century series have been the Reverend Fairchild's, which Miss Hartigan's Cybermen use as an opportunity to suborn the local gentry in *The Next Doctor*, and the informal private ceremonies for the Master and the Doctor in *Last of the Time Lords* and *The Impossible Astronaut*. Of these, one is for a character we never saw alive and the others for recurring characters who are not dead in any permanent sense at all.

Accordingly, when **Doctor Who** makes use of the iconography of human cultural responses to death, it more often serves as a colourful, historical or sinister backdrop than in its authentic, and emotionally essential, function. Tombs are more likely to be cavernous spaces where alien menaces lie dormant than

---

appearing in five, six and nine episodes respectively, compared with Adric's 40 (*Earthshock*, 1982).

reliquaries for the departed (as is the Master's funerary urn which the Doctor is tasked with returning to Gallifrey). Graveyards are sources of information about the past, or venues for sinister surprises like the one Miss Hartigan arranges – although occasionally they serve the former function for the viewer by showing a live character mourning a deceased one[237]. Morgues are invariably places where the dead rise. Funeral parlours and undertakers, where they appear, are played for morbid comedy.

Two stories which deal in detail with the disposal of the dead are *Revelation of the Daleks* and *The Unquiet Dead*, both of them largely set in funeral homes. Though the former apparently takes its inspiration from Evelyn Waugh's post-War satire of American funeral customs, *The Loved One* (1948)[238], and the latter openly from the works of Dickens, both stories end up treating their subject matter similarly, portraying undertakers as ghoulish grotesques and drawing black humour from the physical processes of decomposition. Both stories turn corpses into monsters – respectively Davros's new generation of Daleks and the vehicles of the gaseous Gelth. The parallel with *Dark Water / Death in Heaven* is closer in the case of *Revelation*, where the cryogenically-frozen dead are depicted as conscious, and have their minds subverted rather than their vacated cadavers hijacked. However, *Revelation*, like most of **Doctor Who**'s 1985 season, revels in the potential for body horror (also throwing in cannibalism and vaguely implied

---

[237] We see Clara at her mother's grave in *The Rings of Akhaten*, and Osgood at her duplicate's in *The Zygon Invasion*.
[238] Howe, David, and Stephen James Walker, *Doctor Who: The Television Companion* p483.

necrophilia[239]), and is nihilistically disinterested in transcending this in the way *Death in Heaven* does. *The Unquiet Dead* allows Dickens himself a redemptive ending, but extends no such kindness to the crass undertaker Sneed, let alone the Gelth themselves.

Ben Aaronovitch's two scripts for Sylvester McCoy's seventh Doctor, *Remembrance of the Daleks* and *Battlefield*, are partial exceptions to the series' trivialising of death. While the former does feature an undertaker with a comedy Welsh accent who faints at the sight of a floating coffin – said coffin being, in fact, the disguise for a Gallifreyan super-weapon – the story nonetheless extends a dignity to the dead that *Revelation* denies them. On this occasion the Doctor and Ace duck out just before a funeral, but the final moments at least show us the mourners and coffin (a real one this time) entering the church, and the viewer can, if they wish, imagine the ceremony continuing into the credits. (As in *Black Orchid*, the deceased is not an ally of the Doctor's but a sympathetically portrayed human antagonist, the naïve neo-fascist Mike.) *Battlefield* has the Doctor complain of a nuclear missile's 'graveyard stench', and includes a scene set in a graveyard where the villain Morgaine, on encountering a war memorial, establishes a temporary truce with UNIT's forces to conduct a ceremony honouring the dead. Notably, in each of Aaronovitch's scripts one of the primary villains (the Black Dalek and Morgaine respectively) is talked into submission by an eloquent speech of the Doctor's about the fatal effects of war.

---

[239] See for instance Graham, Jack, 'Sex, Death & Rock 'n' Roll'.

Battlefield also shows the Doctor's grief when he believes his friend the Brigadier has been killed, complicated by his foreknowledge that the Brigadier is 'supposed to die in bed'. *The Wedding of River Song* includes a scene where the 11th Doctor discovers that this has at last happened, and is tempted to give in to despair as a result. Moffat wrote the scene as a tribute to Nicholas Courtney (who died on 22 February 2011, seven months before its broadcast), although he undercuts its solemnity somewhat with the character's post-mortem appearance in *Death in Heaven*.

Though not treating the subject with quite the same seriousness as Aaronovitch, Moffat has shown a greater interest in death and its trappings than most of his peers. Moffat's scripts deploy the iconography of death liberally, as witnessed by the fact that his most prominent additions to **Doctor Who**'s bestiary, the Weeping Angels, are based on funerary statuary. Although his Doctor has remained stubbornly not dead, during Moffat's time as showrunner we have seen his funeral (*The Impossible Astronaut, The Wedding of River Song*), his tomb (*The Name of the Doctor*) and his will (in 2015, beginning with *The Magician's Apprentice*). Moffat's scripts for *Blink* (2007), *The Time of Angels / Flesh and Stone, The Angels Take Manhattan, The Snowmen* and *The Name of the Doctor* all featured scenes in graveyards before *Death in Heaven*'s; *The Witch's Familiar* later shows us the Daleks' unpleasant equivalent.

Because of its particular emphasis on the dead, *Dark Water / Death in Heaven* makes even more extensive use of funereal iconography. As we have already seen, much of this is specific to the theme of wartime remembrance, but the fact that *Dark Water* is set largely in a mausoleum and *Death in Heaven* largely in a cemetery means that memorial imagery is more dominant than in any other **Doctor**

135

Who story, *Revelation of the Daleks* and *The Unquiet Dead* not excepted. Notably, the characters we see who deal with death professionally – Dr Chang at 3W and Graham at the Chaplet Funeral home[240] – are played straight, with none of the earlier stories' gruesome caricature. Our constant awareness of Clara's loss (not to mention Danny's presence during the graveyard scenes) gives a context to this imagery which allows us to ascribe it its real-world connotations of mourning, as well as its genre-drama function as a setting for unnatural resurrections.

While he makes frequent use of its cultural accoutrements, however, and while the fear or anticipation of it looms large in a number of his stories, Moffat's evident respect for death makes him wary of deploying killing as a plot device with too much abandon. His first **Doctor Who** script, *The Empty Child / The Doctor Dances*, famously culminates with the Doctor's joyful declaration that 'Just this once, everybody lives!', but this observation – though it remains unusual in **Doctor Who** as a whole – applies to a number of his other stories, and is even repeated with elaboration by River at the end of *Silence in the Library / Forest of the Dead* ('Now and then, every once in a very long while, every day in a million days, when the wind stands fair and the Doctor comes to call…

---

[240] There is no apparent reason for the funeral home to bear the surname of the first Doctor's companion Dodo Chaplet. (As James Cooray Smith points out in *The Black Archive #2: The Massacre*, the word refers to a rosary prayer, but has no strong funereal connotations.) One guess might be that the name, if it has any significance at all, is present as a rebuke to David Bishop's 1996 tie-in novel *Who Killed Kennedy*, which notoriously killed Dodo off in a brutal subplot, but this feels unsatisfactory.

everybody lives'). His second script, *The Girl in the Fireplace*, contains only one explicit death, and that by natural causes (although the crewmembers whose remnants have been cannibalised offscreen by the *SS Madame de Pompadour* are less likely to have died peacefully). Even the Weeping Angels are – at least when introduced in *Blink* – surprisingly merciful predators, allowing their victims to live out their allotted lifespans in the past, albeit cut off from the lives they knew previously.

While Moffat as showrunner has modified his approach, delivering episodes with considerably higher body counts, his scripts are still notable for their use of carefully constructed get-outs to 'undo' apparent deaths. The earliest of these are the 'nanogenes' in *The Empty Child / The Doctor Dances*, which initially turn their victims into gas-masked zombies – we assume fatally – but ultimately return them all to the bloom of health, even restoring an amputee's leg. Later examples include the rebooting of the entire universe in *The Pandorica Opens / The Big Bang*, which restores everybody swallowed by the cracks in space; the shape-shifting robot with a miniaturised crew which helpfully stands in for the Doctor during his supposed death at Lake Silencio; and the death-ray-powered teleport device which (we will learn in *The Witch's Familiar*) allows Missy to escape her apparent exterminations in *Death in Heaven* and *The Magician's Apprentice*[241].

---

[241] We might also mention the Silurian technology with which Madame Vastra returns Strax and, briefly, Victorian-era Clara to life, but this is less a clever get-out than a straightforward cheat.

137

The number of such evasions is especially prolific for the character of Rory Williams, whose repeatedly undone deaths became a running joke with fans. Moffat acknowledged this in Rory's final story, *The Angels Take Manhattan*, by having him die not once but three times – firstly of old age at the Weeping Angel's human farm in Winter Quay; secondly, jumping to his death from the roof of the same building to avert this future; and thirdly of old age a second time round, after a leftover Weeping Angel sends him back into the past anyway. Though the dramatic timeframe of *The Angels Take Manhattan* is compressed compared with *Dark Water / Death in Heaven*'s, there are intriguing structural parallels with Danny Pink's triple death in the car accident, the mass explosion of the Cyber-army and the final collapse of the Nethersphere. In both cases, the first death introduces a problem which propels the drama, as Rory and Clara struggle to undo what appears to be established fact. The second death is a sacrifice which thwarts the primary threat of the episode, by poisoning the Angels with paradox and diffusing the Cybermen's seeded rainclouds. The third rights an earlier wrong inflicted on another party, in allowing Amy to live out the remainder of her life with Rory, and Danny's former victim to return from the dead. The sacrificial element of this – in both cases averting a pseudo-supernatural danger, whether in the form of angels or the spirits of the dead – recalls ancient European rituals of propitiation in which (according to both archaeological and mythological evidence) a victim would suffer a 'threefold death' of wounding, strangulation and drowning to appease the gods[242].

---

[242] Spangenberg, Lisa L, 'Did the Celts or Druids Perform Human Sacrifice?'

138

Given the dissimilarity with the types of death Danny and Rory suffer, though, this is unlikely to be significant.

While Moffat displays the narrative tic with unusual frequency, the death-that-turns-out-not-to-be is also hardly unusual for an action-adventure series, and for **Doctor Who** in particular. Many of the series' cliffhangers rely on apparently fatal events which prove on further inspection to have been not so very fatal, while villains like the Master and Davros have long been capable of reappearing after apparently unambiguous deaths onscreen. The Doctor's regenerations have often been treated like deaths (most explicitly in The End of Time where we are told: 'Even if I change, it feels like dying. Everything I am dies.'), and yet his adventures continue. Peri's apparent death is undone, as are those of Grace and Chang Lee[243]. The ultimate expression of this tendency is not Rory but Captain Jack who, once restored to life by Rose during her Bad Wolf apotheosis, becomes explicitly incapable of dying (although the actual mechanics of this vary wildly based on plot convenience)[244].

Of the main characters in Dark Water / Death in Heaven, the Doctor and Missy are thus impervious to death; Clara has died in at least two iterations (and presumably many more) as a result of her

---

[243] The Trial of a Time Lord episodes 8 and 14, Doctor Who (1996).
[244] The Parting of the Ways, Utopia, The Sound of Drums / Last of the Time Lords, Journey's End and throughout **Torchwood**. The inconsistency is seen most starkly in Utopia, where an electric shock kills Jack in the usual manner before he returns to life a short while later, but he later remains alive and active in a radiation field which vaporises normal human flesh.

scattering across the Doctor's timeline in *The Name of the Doctor*, and will later escape an apparently final death, at least temporarily, thanks to Gallifreyan technology[245]; and Osgood dies in this story but leaves behind a duplicate (or original) who acts like her and is able to recruit a duplicate of her own[246]. None of these survivals and resurrections are even connected to the main conceit of the story, the Nethersphere, which brings back Danny, the Brigadier and the nameless boy. This mechanism is of a kind which Moffat has used before; indeed, he introduced it in a script for the 10th Doctor before he became showrunner, *Silence in the Library / Forest of the Dead*.

If **Doctor Who** has been understandably reticent about the experience of bereavement, it has shown even less interest in the aftermath of death from the point of view of the deceased. Prior to *Deep Breath*, there had been virtually no suggestion in **Doctor Who** that there might be an afterlife, except in the beliefs of a handful of characters[247]. When Heaven is invoked, it is generally as a mild oath

---

[245] As seen in *Asylum of the Daleks* and *The Snowmen*, and *Hell Bent*.

[246] As revealed in *The Zygon Invasion / The Zygon Inversion*.

[247] **Torchwood** is more forthright on the matter, stating a number of times that death is experienced as an empty void, although one can delay entering it or be restored from it by the intervention of certain alien technologies (*Everything Changes*, *They Keep Killing Suzie*, *Random Shoes* (all 2006) et al). This is of particular interest since **Torchwood** draws heavily on the continuity of *The Unquiet Dead*, where (in one of **Doctor Who**'s very few examples of apparent post-death survival) Gwyneth continues to speak and act under her own control for some minutes after physical death. Although Dickens cheerfully attributes this to the supernatural, in

('Good heavens', 'For heaven's sake,' 'Thank heavens'), or more rarely a mock-archaic reference to the sky. 'Hell' is normally just a slightly stronger oath (generally in the 21st-century stories), though it is also mentioned as an abode of demons (for instance in *The King's Demons* and *Battlefield*), and Rita theorises that the prison ship in *The God Complex* (2011) is Jahannam, the Islamic equivalent. *Planet of the Spiders* uses the Buddhist understanding of reincarnation as a metaphor for Time Lord regeneration – and possibly vice-versa – and *Kinda* (1982) alludes to the same idea when the shaman Panna transfers herself telepathically into her apprentice's mind at the point of death.

Of the Doctor's companions, the only one to state definite beliefs concerning an afterlife is Katarina, and those (that she is already dead following the fall of Troy, and the Doctor is conducting her through the Underworld to a 'place of perfection') are ruled out by the audience's knowledge, even before they are catastrophically disproven by her decompressive death in a spaceship airlock. A brief line in *Doctor Who* (1996) suggests that the eighth Doctor thinks of death as a place that can be explored: 'Well, you've both been somewhere I've never been. Congratulations.' (Grace's reply that 'It's nothing to be scared of' is uninformative.) Although the Doctor says in *Dark Water* that 'Almost every culture in the universe has some concept of an afterlife. I always meant to have a look around, see if I could find one,' we have seen little previous

---

the light of later developments it seems more likely to be just the sort of thing that happens in Cardiff.

141

sign of such an interest. He will later confess to a fear of dying, but claim not to be scared of Hell[248].

From *Deep Breath* to *Dark Water*, the Nethersphere is unambiguously described as the afterlife, implying that it is, definitively and cosmically, the place where people's souls go when they die. The audience is free not to believe this, of course, but it is only with *Dark Water*'s visual transition between Missy's hovering sphere (unidentified at this point, but clearly alien technology) and Danny and Seb in the interior of the spherical city that any hint is given of the more complex truth. Whether or not there is indeed an afterlife in the **Doctor Who** universe, the Nethersphere is (it transpires) merely a technological artefact into which the consciousnesses which Missy has harvested have been uploaded (though there are evidently many of them, and Missy implies that all the human dead are there[249]). This truth is crystallised in Missy's comment that 'You know, it's ever so funny, the people that live inside that think they've gone to Heaven.'

The Nethersphere is a 'Matrix data slice... Time Lord technology,'[250] and the parent Matrix of which it is presumably a cutting has been a known aspect of Time Lord society since *The Deadly Assassin*. As

---

[248] *Heaven Sent.*

[249] 'You know the key strategic weakness of the human race? The dead outnumber the living.' [*Dark Water*]. Since 'the dead' are not a constant subset of humanity but are continually growing in number, Missy is presumably referring to the dead of the story's present day, especially since they all apparently have bodies to go back to. (We have, however, seen her collect one soul, Gretchen, from the future.)

[250] *Dark Water.*

Co-ordinator Engin then explained the principle: 'The cells are the repository of departed Time Lords. At the moment of death an electrical scan is made of the brain pattern, and these millions of impulses are immediately transferred...' Though the Doctor refers to 'brain cells', Engin corrects him to 'Trillions of electrochemical cells in a continuous Matrix', implying that the computation substrate is technological, not biological. In any case, the SF concept is that which has become known as the 'uploaded consciousness' or 'upload' for short, defined in *The Encyclopedia of Science Fiction* (ESF) as 'the copying or transfer of a human or other personality to a sentient software representation'[251]. Although the Matrix is described in terms of the Time Lords' survival after death, it is experienced by the Doctor – who is plugged into it when still alive – as a virtual environment, in which he meets no-one else except the equally alive Chancellor Goth. Later stories including *Arc of Infinity* and 'The Ultimate Foe' similarly depict the Matrix as a subjective environment, but omit to show the experience of the deceased Time Lords who supposedly inhabit it. (*Hell Bent* shows us that some of them are weaponised as 'Cloister Wraiths', and the Doctor describes the setup succinctly as 'a big computer made of ghosts, in a crypt guarded by more ghosts'.)

This contrasts with the approach of the only 20th-century **Doctor Who** story to feature uploads directly, *Four to Doomsday* (1982). In this, the minds of humans collected by aliens in variously distant (and in some cases totally invented) historical periods have been coded onto computer chips and placed in android bodies. The

---

[251] Langford, David, and Brian M Stableford, 'Upload'.

Urbankans apply the practice to themselves, allowing them to appear human rather than toadlike by simply transferring their chip to a new mechanical host. *Four to Doomsday* does not give its artificial souls a virtual heaven, instead placing them on a very physical spaceship ruled by the megalomaniac Monarch. While Monarch apparently believes that he is the creator of the universe, and at least one of the androids, Kurkutji, believes that their destination is the Dreamtime (a complex concept in Indigenous Australian animism dubiously translated by Tegan as 'Heaven'), the religious aspects of the situation are played down, in favour of the rationalism espoused by the uploaded Greek philosopher Bigon.

The first **Doctor Who** story which directly marries the idea of consciousness uploads with that of virtual reality (a combination which, as ESF describes, has long since become a staple in SF literature, though it is rarer in media SF) is Moffat's *Silence in the Library / Forest of the Dead*. In this, Donna Noble becomes one of thousands individuals 'saved' from death (a play on words linking the storing of computer files with the religious concept of salvation) to a virtual environment where she is able to live out a comforting fantasy of domestic life with a husband and children. This heaven has a presiding deity in its original upload, the young girl for whom it was created, known as CAL. While the afterlife Donna temporarily lives there is believable as her ideal, and even CAL's, it seems a less perfect match for River Song, who ends up inhabiting it after her own, seemingly permanent, death. (*The Name of the Doctor* suggests that she is not necessarily confined there, however.)

A couple of hints in later Moffat scripts suggest that his futuristic, militarised church and its rivals may use a similar arrangement to

144

create afterlives for their dead, but the reference to 'heaven-neutral' territories in *A Good Man Goes to War* and the comment that 'The relevant afterlives have been notified' in *The Time of the Doctor* are fleeting compared with even the early scenes set in the Nethersphere during the 2014 season.

In *The Deadly Assassin* the environment of the Matrix changes based on the demands of its occupants, and from what we see the virtual reality of the Nethersphere is also an inconsistent environment. The sunny garden with its antique stone colonnades where we first see Missy is difficult to reconcile with the apparently all-encompassing modern night-time cityscape which Seb shows Danny, and beyond the fact that the indefinitely-extending corridor where Seb greets CSO Matthew curves noticeably upwards towards its ends, as it would in the interior of a hollow sphere, there is no clear consistency between these various settings. It is relatively easy to accept the garden where Missy receives the Half-Face Man as a manifestation of Heaven, and the hotel dining-room overlooking a different sunny garden where she takes tea with Gretchen as part of the same geography – but these are the new arrivals Missy makes the effort to welcome personally, and there is reason to think that they may be getting special treatment. We see only the first seconds of her meeting with Gretchen, but she is keen to pump the Half-Face Man for information about her 'boyfriend'. From Matthew's arrival onwards the Nethersphere takes on a colder, more bureaucratic aspect[252]. Seb's corporate office feels

---

[252] Missy's appearances in *Flatline* and *In the Forest of the Night* show us little of her surroundings, but it seems likely that they take place in the 3W facility rather than the Nethersphere: certainly the

like a suitable setting for the Kafkaesque conversation in which he persuades Danny that he is dead, and the view from his balcony is, at least, an unorthodox one of Heaven.

(This is not to say that the traditional Heaven is never portrayed as a city. Indeed, this image informs Christian depictions of Heaven from St Augustine to *The Pilgrim's Progress*, and dates back at least to the biblical book of *Revelation*. It may even be deliberate that the Nethersphere, like the Bible, begins in a garden and ends in a city. The 'New Jerusalem' St John describes in *Revelation* could plausibly lack a sun or moon, as the city version of the Nethersphere seems to; in *Revelation*, however, 'the city had no need of the sun, neither of the moon, to shine in it: for the glory of God did lighten it,'[253] whereas the Nethersphere has no apparent light source beyond the electricity of its streets and buildings. In other respects, John's walled, gated and bejewelled city has little visual commonality with Moffat's.)

Seb and Missy may bandy about terms like 'Heaven', 'the Promised Land' and 'Paradise', but these would be more convincing in the mouths of characters other than an archvillain and her henchman. All the scenes featuring the dead are inductions into the afterlife – an extended one, in Danny's case – and aside from Danny and the unspeaking boy (who has presumably been resident in the

---

lighting in the former matches 3W's, and she uses a tablet to watch the events of both these episodes, rather than the hovering holographic window through which she observes the Doctor's fall in *Death in Heaven*.
[253] *Revelation* 21:23.

146

Nethersphere for some years), we follow none of them beyond their initial post-death scenes. This makes it impossible to know anything of their long-term existences, beyond the horrific allegation that their comfort depends on the good treatment of their vacated cadaver, and the equally chilling fact that they can all be assumed to end up as Cybermen, neither of which are particularly paradisiacal experiences. Whereas CAL was a benevolent divinity, concerned to safeguard the welfare of the souls she rescued, Missy's purpose for the Nethersphere is seemingly to condition the dead to become animating intelligences for Cybermen. It might be more accurate to interpret the Nethersphere, not as a Paradise but as the Cybermen's equivalent of Purgatory, cleansing its occupants of emotion to fit them for their coming elevated state.

There is another option, of course. The other term Seb uses for the Nethersphere is 'the Underworld', and in the cityscape's interiority, its apparently perpetual darkness and its ruler's lack of interest in human concerns, it is akin to the classical afterlife that Katarina (or at least the later Greek poets who wrote about the Trojans of her era) would have recognised. Thanks to the influence of that classical belief system, it also recalls the traditional Christian depiction of Hell.

The Doctor's suggestion that Clara should 'Go to Hell' feels flippant, partly because it is written to be misunderstood and partly because our current consensual morality would not consign Danny to such a destination[254]. Clearly, though, for Danny the experience of being haunted by the boy he killed is a hellish one, and Hell, too, has been depicted as a city – notably by Dante Alighieri, whose *Inferno* located it physically inside the sphere of the Earth and incorporated into its description many aspects of the classical Underworld. Certainly, Clara's mission to rescue Danny makes more sense, and is less selfish, if she believes him in Hell, not in Heaven.

If the Nethersphere is the Underworld, then Clara intends to play Orpheus to Danny's Eurydice – saving her partner from a senseless death by reclaiming his soul from the rulers of the afterlife. If it is the Christian Hell, then perhaps it is Danny who is the mythic figure, re-enacting on a smaller scale the Harrowing of Hell – Jesus's rescue of the virtuous souls of the past, taking place between the crucifixion and resurrection – in saving this one innocent victim. In either case, the final departure of the souls preserved within this limited and partial afterlife is no tragedy to be mourned, but a merciful release for all concerned.

---

[254] Strictly orthodox interpretations of Christianity would, of course – since Danny has no apparent religious faith, is presumably sleeping with Clara despite their not being married, and dies unexpectedly with no opportunity to repent his unbelief and fornication – but this is likely to trouble only a minority of the audience, in the UK at least.

CHAPTER 6. 'CYBERMEN FROM CYBERSPACE': IS THIS CYBERPUNK?

Dark Water is not the first episode of **Doctor Who** to use the term 'cyberspace'; nor (despite Missy's 'Now, why has no-one ever thought of that before?') is it the first to relate it to the Cybermen. Given how prevalent the word has become in the 21st century, though, her utterance has surprisingly few precedents.

The English word originates in William Gibson's 1982 short story 'Burning Chrome'[255], although the quote most often used in defining it comes from his best-known novel *Neuromancer* (1984):

> 'A consensual hallucination experienced daily by billions of legitimate operators, in every nation, by children being taught mathematical concepts... A graphic representation of data abstracted from the banks of every computer in the human system.'[256]

Doctor Who's *The Deadly Assassin* predates *Neuromancer* by eight years: intriguingly, Gibson's main synonym for 'cyberspace' (and one which has had almost equal cultural penetration thanks to its appropriation for the Wachowskis' blockbuster film of the same name) is 'the matrix'[257].

---

[255] Gibson, William, *Burning Chrome and Other Stories*, p195. It was previously used in Danish for a style of installation art (Lillemose, Jacob and Matthias Kryger, 'The (Re)invention of Cyberspace').
[256] Gibson, William, *Neuromancer* p67.
[257] For instance, Gibson, *Neuromancer* pp11-12.

Doctor Who has always dabbled in illusory environments of one kind and another, the earliest being Morphoton in 'The Velvet Web' (*The Keys of Marinus* episode 2, 1964). The kind of 'consensual hallucination' we call virtual reality or VR (which refers specifically to immersive, interactive, computer-generated environments) is a variant of this concept based on information technology rather than drugs, hypnosis or magic. In 20th-century **Doctor Who** VR appears solely (and inconsistently[258]) in the context of the Time Lords' Matrix, and the technology remains rare in the 21st-century programme, although arguable examples include the disguised settings of *The God Complex* and *Mummy on the Orient Express*. *Nightmare in Silver* (2013) establishes a precedent for the association of Cybermen with such environments (though the term 'cyberspace' is not used) by using a VR as the venue for the Doctor's struggle with the Cyberplanner personality attempting to take him over.

Steven Moffat's scripts show a recurring interest in illusory realities: in *Dark Water* itself, the Doctor imposes a hypnotic hallucination on Clara which is wholly unrelated to the story's primary unreal environment, the Nethersphere[259]. Some of these can legitimately be considered VRs, such as Kazran's immersive

---

[258] Pip and Jane Baker seem to struggle with the concept: in 'The Ultimate Foe' the Matrix is entered through a physical door, and the Master parks his TARDIS there. This suggests that the Matrix is more like an artificial pocket universe, like the interior of a TARDIS, than a true VR.
[259] Clara seems to make a habit of finding herself in such imagined spaces: see *Asylum of the Daleks*, *The Name of the Doctor*, *Last Christmas* and *The Zygon Inversion* for further examples.

experience via hologram of the spaceship in *A Christmas Carol*. Another such is CAL's virtual heaven in *Silence in the Library / Forest of the Dead*, which is identified as 'cyberspace' in a piece of wordplay which recalls Missy's 'Cybermen from cyberspace': when Donna asks why her children are identical to everyone else's, her fellow upload Miss Evangelista explains, 'It saves an awful lot of space,' then clarifies that she means 'Cyberspace'[260].

The much-quoted lines from *Neuromancer* go on to describe the visual appearance of the matrix as being 'like city lights, receding,' which describes what we literally see during the big reveal in *Dark Water*[261]. In *Neuromancer*, though, the matrix merely **looks** like city lights: it does not simulate them. While 'cyberspace' has come to describe any VR environment, Gibson's usage is more specific: the environment described in *Neuromancer* is created as a concrete visual metaphor for the data and processes which exist in all networked computers. It is thus functional without being representational: more like an immersive, indefinitely extended 3D user desktop than the setting of a realistic computer game. Of all the VRs in 21st-century **Doctor Who**, Gaiman's is the only one which does not directly mimic reality, and certainly Moffat's VR afterlives are cyberspaces only in this approximate sense.

Admittedly **Doctor Who**'s earliest use of the term is looser still. In *Rise of the Cybermen / The Age of Steel* (2006) John Lumic, creator of the Cybermen in that story's alternative history, refers to the conversion process as 'the ultimate upgrade... our greatest step

---

[260] *Forest of the Dead.*
[261] *Neuromancer* p67.

151

into cyberspace.' Unlike the two uses in Moffat scripts, there is no indication that this refers to a consensual virtual reality, and Lumic seems to be employing the term rhetorically, as a buzzword suggesting merely that humanity is to become more advanced. In fact (as becomes apparent when Lumic's publicity video is replayed later in *Rise of the Cybermen*) Tom Macrae's script is using it primarily to justify the modifying prefix in the name 'Cybermen', preparatory to identifying the eponymous monsters for the first time in the 21st century.

On their appearances between 1966 and 1987, the name referred to the Cybermen's identity as cybernetic organisms[262] – 'cyborgs' – but the proliferation of 'cyber-' as a prefix towards the end of the 20th century justified (and perhaps required) a more populist meaning. This linguistic change was partly driven by the rapidly increasing availability, accessibility and usefulness of computer technology itself, but also by the popularity of 'cyberpunk', a subgenre of and cultural movement arising from SF, as one of whose founders Gibson is generally credited.

Cyberpunk is a complex cultural phenomenon defying simplistic definitions, but most discussions concentrate on the tension

---

[262] This is stated explicitly in *The Tenth Planet* episode 2:
        KRAIL
    We are called Cybermen.
        BARCLAY
    Cybermen?
        KRAIL
    Yes, Cybermen. We were exactly like you once, but our cybernetic scientists realised that our race was getting weak.

between the 'cyber' element of the name – referring to hyperconnected, information-heavy futures reliant on computer networks, and frequently embodied in virtual reality environments – with the 'punk' element, representing political awareness and countercultural rebellion[263]. While the worlds of cyberpunk SF are dominated by corporations as monolithic as the skyscrapers which loom over their cityscapes, the characters typically operate at ground level, a downtrodden underclass struggling – and usually failing – to subvert or collapse the corporations' technologies through desperate experimentation. Cyberpunk's protagonists tend to be alienated and dislocated, its futures short-term and its vision global. Its worlds are inhabited by an eclectic mix of displaced cultures and ethnicities, with any necessary mythic or religious touchpoints provided by marginalised minority faiths like Rastafarianism and voodoo. Its standard repertoire of technological imagery includes artificial intelligences, brain-computer interfaces, designer drugs, body modification (whether cybernetic, surgical or genetic), and, above all, virtual reality – all of them tending to erase the boundaries between humanity and its technologies. In contrast to the perfectibility of its VR environments, its physical realities are often squalid, rickety and rundown, dominated by intrusive advertising media: although made too early to be a cyberpunk text, the film *Blade Runner* (1982) has been a seminal influence on the way cyberpunk looks.

Cyberpunk's popularity peaked during the late 1980s and early 1990s, falling off once networked computers became a mundane

---

[263] See for instance Nicholls, Peter, 'Cyberpunk'.

element of daily life. During this time, televised **Doctor Who** was largely off the air, meaning that the movement's influence on **Doctor Who** is most strongly visible in the tie-in media of these years, and in particular in Virgin Publishing's **Doctor Who: The New Adventures** novels. These can be seen as an aspect of the same early-90s boom in British SF which produced the formative works of writers such as Stephen Baxter, Paul J McAuley and Alastair Reynolds[264]. The books represent a sustained – though perhaps ultimately unsustainable – effort to reinvent **Doctor Who** as a literary rather than a televisual phenomenon, and the best of them are literate, morally complex, politically aware and adult[265]. Among them are unquestionably works of cyberpunk: in *Cat's Cradle: Warhead* (1992), for instance, written by the 20th-century series' final script editor Andrew Cartmel, the Doctor and Ace roam a near-future Earth whose societies are collapsing as its technologies proliferate, assembling the human components of a weapon to take down a wealthy global corporation[266]; while *Transit* (1992), by *Remembrance of the Daleks* and *Battlefield*'s scriptwriter Ben Aaronovitch, sees an interplanetary mass transport network

---

[264] All three of whom have since written works of **Doctor Who** prose fiction, although none of them contributed to **The New Adventures**: McAuley's *Eye of the Tyger* (2003), Baxter's *The Wheel of Ice* (2012) and Reynolds's *Harvest of Time* (2013).

[265] This is not to deny that the worst of them can be adolescent, politically naïve, morally offensive and borderline illiterate.

[266] Cartmel's sequels, *Warlock* (1995) and *Warchild* (1996), retreat from this bleak but compelling future, to the extent that the last, set more than two decades after the first, depicts a world little different from the then present day.

develop sentience and begin reprogramming the disenfranchised underclass of the solar system's ethnically diverse, genetically and cybernetically enhanced population.

A multicultural global sensibility and a broadly leftwing politics emerged from such early books to become staples of **The New Adventures**, and many later titles in the series embrace cyberpunk motifs such as experimental drugs, engagement with countercultures, obscure religious beliefs and – with great frequency – virtual reality. Contributors to the novel series included future **Doctor Who** scriptwriters Paul Cornell, Mark Gatiss, Matt Jones, Gareth Roberts and Russell T Davies[267] – whose *Damaged Goods* (1996), though set in the near past of the 1980s rather than the near future, shows a similar concern with urban alienation and social collapse, augmented drugs, and the merging of humanity and technology.

While VR is a major touchstone of cyberpunk, the genre's detailed characteristics are complex. In the absence of a clear definition, comparing *Dark Water / Death in Heaven* with the traits listed above yields mixed results.

The erasure of boundaries between humanity and technology, and the specific concept of body-modification, are clearly present in the story's Cybermen (though given their smooth and gleaming lines this is mostly apparent in *Death in Heaven*, when Danny breaches

---

[267] Moffat was not a direct participant, although he contributed the short story 'Continuity Errors' to Lane, Andy and Justin Richards, eds, *Decalog 3*, an anthology published by Virgin and using the **New Adventures** continuity.

155

his helmet's integrity to reveal his ravaged face). Seb is described by Missy as 'an AI interface', meaning that he is not himself one of the uploaded dead. Some kind of hands-off brain-computer interface must exist to enable the uploading, but this is not shown directly. The Doctor's 'sleep patch things' are the nearest the story comes to designer drugs, and their technological basis is not discussed[268]. The world depicted, with its instant access to global information sources, obviously echoes the hyperconnected networked futures of cyberpunk; but technology and culture have moved on since the 1980s, to the extent that this is one of *Dark Water / Death in Heaven*'s realistic elements, a mundane depiction of the story's present. The story does depict the imaginary use of such networks to communicate with the dead, although this is a feature of Missy's Gallifreyan technology rather than an indication that the story takes place in the near future.

Politically, corporations and the mega-rich are present in the story, in the form of 3W and its supposed clientele, but are not its focus; and since 3W's terrestrial base is in St Paul's, their standard filmic signifier – the nightscape of brightly-lit skyscrapers echoing the opening of *Blade Runner* – exists only in the VR of the Nethersphere. Cultural pluralism is not in evidence (all the speaking characters of whatever ethnicity being apparently British, and generally defined by their jobs rather than their background); and for all that the Doctor notionally becomes president of the world, the awareness of culture outside Britain is effectively confined to Missy's perfunctory list of global cities (including Glasgow).

---

[268] *Dark Water.*

Indeed, the Doctor's presidential power and his military connections represent a substantial obstacle to considering the story as cyberpunk, whose protagonists are typically marginalised and powerless. Of his human allies, the most alienated is probably Osgood, and her issues are far more personal than political. Considering Danny as such a protagonist is perhaps more promising: although his life before death was as comfortably middle-class as Clara's, as a mechanically-augmented walking corpse he must now be considered cut off from mainstream society. He does, however, have a whole new hive-mind to join along with all the other augmented human dead, so can hardly be considered isolated. More significantly, in political terms, a teacher with a military background is unlikely to speak for any counterculture. As discussed in Chapters two and three, Danny's elevation to command of the Cyber-army represents a revolution of sorts, but it is an abstract and theoretical one compared with cyberpunk's more visceral concerns.

There is, in effect, a fundamental philosophical mismatch between cyberpunk's approach and that of **Doctor Who**: the former's frequently cynical pessimism, its persistent worry that human beings are little more than accidentally self-aware pieces of organic machinery, and its conviction that ordinary people can change their worlds in minor, incremental ways at best, are fundamentally at odds with **Doctor Who**'s habitual optimism, its humanism and – most obviously – the repeated epic victories of its central character. Separately (and less to **Doctor Who**'s credit), there is a tension between cyberpunk's global perspective and the idiosyncratic and occasionally blinkered patriotism which the series has sometimes displayed under Moffat[269]. A cyberpunk story is an aberration in **Doctor Who** terms, which may explain some of the hostility shown towards **The New Adventures** by many 1990s **Doctor Who** fans.

Is it fair, though, to say that *Dark Water / Death in Heaven* is the closest televised **Doctor Who** has come to this SF subgenre? Actually, probably not. Early in the 21st-century revival, Russell T Davies contributed a story focussing on malign corporate influences, media broadcast through ubiquitous screens and direct brain-computer interfaces, and the power of information to change the world. It features no VR technology, but in other respects is a closer match for cyberpunk than perhaps any other televised **Doctor Who** story.

The Long Game's interest in networks, body modification and brain-computer interfaces, and its erasure of the boundaries between humanity and technology, are prominently visible in its depiction of 'info-spike' technology. This is a hinged portal in the skull whereby information (visible from the outside as streams of blue energy – we are not privy to the experiences of the user) can directly enter the brain, allowing a human being to become a component in the gigantic broadcasting machine that is Satellite Five. The story also shows us more familiar information conduits, in the form of television broadcasts and mobile phone connections,

---

[269] The clearest example of which is the unquestioningly positive portrayal of Winston Churchill in *The Beast Below*, *Victory of the Daleks* and *The Wedding of River Song*.

and suggests for the first time in a TV story that leaked information about the future can be as significant a danger to the stability of history as physical time-travel. Its setting is notionally the far rather than the near future[270], but the scope of the information sources it depicts is global as well as interplanetary, taking in not only the New Venus Archipelago but also Morocco and – as it happens – Glasgow.

The Long Game is also interested in politics, and can be the more confident about it for not having to rely on Davies's shaky grasp of the specifics of contemporary government. Here, too, there is little sign of multiculturalism – but this is explained by humanity being conditioned to become a monoculture by the media manipulations of the Jagrafess and the Editor, whose stranglehold on humanity is as firm as their unnamed company's control over the lives of its staff of Satellite Five. These villains are inherently corporate in their operations and ideology, rather than simply finding a corporation convenient to achieve their ends. Their only opponent who we see is an undercover paramilitary freedom fighter who understands that 'This whole system is corrupt'; an armed anarchist hopelessly outgunned by the Editor's superior grasp of information.

Perhaps most crucially, in contrast to *Dark Water / Death in Heaven*, we see the experiences of the ordinary people on Satellite Five. The skyscrapers and gleaming corridors of Moffat's

---

[270] Although typically of Davies's futures, the date of 200,000 CE is an arbitrary round number, and there is no effort to realistically portray the extreme historical distance of a fifth of a million years – 40,000 times longer than the entire history of human civilisation to date.

Nethersphere, unlike those of *Blade Runner* and its cyberpunk successors, are contrasted with no ground-level views of everyday life in the afterlife: we see no dirt, no mess, no ugly functionality. By contrast, *The Long Game* depicts an untidy, cluttered future where space stations suffer air-conditioning malfunctions and food-stall owners fry up on the concourse, offering such hybrid cuisine as beef-flavoured slush puppies. A word often used in describing cyberpunk's lived-in futures (perhaps for its incorporation of the word 'grim' as well as its overtones of grease and grittiness) is 'grimy': the shooting script for *The Long Game* goes so far as to call the speaking stallholder 'GRIMY MAN'[271].

It is often difficult to tell how far 21st-century TV **Doctor Who** has been influenced specifically by **The New Adventures**, rather than by general trends in science fiction between 1989 and 2005. In the case of scripts written by **New Adventures** authors, the presumption should perhaps be that influence is present, but *The Long Game*'s indebtedness is more visible than in any story save *Human Nature / The Family of Blood*.

One effect of incorporating a strongly heroic character into cyberpunk narratives was that **The New Adventures** (and Cartmel's novels in particular) were frequently seen as marginalising or disempowering the Doctor. As discussed in Chapter two, the ninth Doctor's relative impotence is an important part of his character development, and the fact (revealed in *Bad Wolf*) that his actions in *The Long Game* ultimately make no difference to the condition of the corporate drones and their peers, is certainly suggestive. More

---

[271] Davies, Russell T, et al, *Doctor Who: The Shooting Scripts*, p240.

so is the fact that the episode's five-minute central confrontation between the Editor and Suki – also the centrepiece of this Doctor's character arc, given *The Long Game*'s pivotal position in the season – is one which he is not present at or even aware of at the time. The smoking gun, however, is the script's reference to the near-future 'Butler Corporation', which strongly recalls (and may be a misremembering of) 'the Butler Institute', the corporate villains of *Cat's Cradle: Warhead*[272].

The Long Game is not an aberration, though it and its sequel *Bad Wolf* are Davies's most visibly cyberpunk-influenced scripts. *Gridlock* (2007) draws on similar motifs and adds designer drugs and social collapse, while most of his contemporary Earth stories involve global communications, short-term projections of current technology, and some degree of societal breakdown.

This is not to deny that *Dark Water / Death in Heaven* is influenced by cyberpunk, or indeed by the **New Adventures**; nor to suggest that its debt to them comes via Davies-era **Doctor Who**, rather than from Moffat's own reading. Other scripts of Moffat's manifest some of the cyberpunk traits which are absent in *Dark Water / Death in Heaven*: mind-computer interfaces appear in *The Bells of Saint John* (where Miss Kizlet's human employees are as much computer peripherals as her AI 'servers'), while *Time Heist* shows criminals augmented by unreliable technologies trying to undermine a wealthy corporation. *The Beast Below* employs a

---

[272] Davies, *The Shooting Scripts*, p258 (the scene was cut from the broadcast episode). The Butler Institute building in New York can be seen briefly in a later Davies-era episode, *The Poison Sky* (2008).

similar cluttered, crowded aesthetic to *The Long Game*'s, and accompanies it with a similar awareness of the drudgery of the oppressed. Even so, *Dark Water / Death in Heaven* remains Moffat's most overtly cyberpunk script, and Missy's wordplay is no empty name-check. Nonetheless, this comparison shows that one popular perception of 21st-century **Doctor Who**'s first two showrunners – that it is Moffat who is more interested in science fiction's scope for storytelling, while Davies takes more of his inspiration from soap opera and reality TV – is an oversimplification.

Another fallacy sometimes encountered – that Moffat is the more dour and cynical of the two, while Davies has a cuddlier, more jovial view of the universe – seems to be based more on the personalities both men project in interviews than on the contents of their scripts. In his writing Moffat is a sentimentalist: as previously outlined, he was writing **Doctor Who** for four years before he begin killing off his characters, and as of 2015 he is still undoing their deaths[273]. His nearest approaches to dystopia, *The Beast Below* and *A Christmas Carol*, are dissolved when the characters responsible for creating them repent[274]. He is the showrunner who would have us believe Santa Claus is real, rather than a murderous alien robot.

By contrast, Davies's ironically named *Utopia* and *Last of the Time Lords* expect humanity to end its days in degradation and despair; *Turn Left* and *Midnight* (both 2008) present the failure of human

---

[273] *The Girl Who Died, Heaven Sent, Hell Bent.*
[274] Liz 10 and Kazran Sardick respectively.

integrity in extremis as mercilessly as any Terry Nation script; and *Damaged Goods* – written for an adult readership without concession to the expectations of a Saturday-evening family audience – is one of the bleakest **Doctor Who** stories in any medium.

The contrast between cyberpunk's ethos and that of **Doctor Who** is a real one, but it may be that Davies's sometimes savage pessimism makes him better suited to bridge that gap than his cheerier successor.

CONCLUSION: 'SO, WHAT NOW?'

Chapter one of this study began with the fairly mundane observation that *Dark Water / Death in Heaven* is 'profoundly a work of series drama, located firmly within a continuing narrative'. This was obviously true at the time of broadcast, but has become ever more inescapable with the benefit of a year's worth (and counting) of hindsight.

The first inklings of inspiration for the **Black Archive** series came in January 2015, when the most recent **Doctor Who** story to air was *Last Christmas*, and *Dark Water / Death in Heaven* was fresh in the memory. This text was finalised a year later, shortly after the broadcast of *The Husbands of River Song*. During that time, the broadcast of the 13 episodes from *The Magician's Apprentice* to *The Husbands of River Song* have significantly altered many of the things this study originally intended to say.

For instance, Chapter two originally assumed – despite the fact that neither Moffat nor the Master is celebrated for their unstinting honesty – that Missy's plans for Clara had been played out in *Death in Heaven*, and that the question would not be reopened in the 2015 season. This idea began to seem untenable at the time of *The Witch's Familiar*, and was definitively shot down by *Hell Bent*.

Similarly, in early November 2014, *Death in Heaven*'s Remembrance Day imagery could only be interpreted in the light of Moffat's World War II scripts, with their patriotic praise for the 'tiny, damp little island [that] says "No",' and their warnings that

'That's right Adolf, the British are coming!'[275]. In early November 2015, the political polemic of *The Zygon Inversion*, co-written by Moffat, retrospectively recast this whole sequence as a distinctly more sceptical statement about the value of celebrating wars.

Thirdly, an early draft of Chapter one, observing that *Dark Water / Death in Heaven* came closer to the Tennant-era formula for ending a season than any of the Matt Smith stories, speculated that each of the regular 21st-century Doctors – Eccleston, Tennant, Smith and Capaldi – might have their own characteristic style of finale. By entirely failing to conform to that model, *Face the Raven*, *Heaven Sent* and *Hell Bent* (however one classifies them in terms of story structure, which is in itself part of their deviation) forcefully ended that line of speculation.

So, as the season progressed, new episodes provided multiple new insights: a deepening understanding of Missy's character; a further example of **Doctor Who**'s treatment of survival after death; a new enigmatic, morally ambivalent woman on the margins of the Doctor's life; a radical recontextualising of 21st-century UNIT continuity; the final culmination of Clara's character arc; a second gender-switching regeneration taking place before our eyes; the final culmination of Clara's character arc again. The fact that 11 of the 13 episodes broadcast in 2015 are cited in this book is not due to a desperate search for up-to-date relevance, but because each of them has affected, sometimes profoundly, some element of the interpretation of *Dark Water / Death in Heaven*. Other stories have had their contexts similarly changed: a line in *Deep Breath*, a

---

[275] *The Empty Child, Let's Kill Hitler.*

relationship in 'The Night of the Doctor', a major character in *Genesis of the Daleks* (1975), the entire premise of *An Unearthly Child* (1963), all look different now if we choose to see them that way. (Even *Face the Raven* will never again be the story it was during those heady days between 21 November and 5 December 2015.)

This recontextualisation of the past can be seen as particularly characteristic of Moffat's tenure as showrunner, but it is scarcely unique to this era. Since 2010 we have twice visited the Doctor's life prior to *An Unearthly Child*[276], something that had never previously been seen on TV; we have learned why he 'really' fled Gallifrey[277], and that the TARDIS believes she chose him as her pilot[278]. Still, such revelations were hardly off-limits previously: during the Pertwee era we discovered that the Doctor had been an activist on his home planet[279], learned that planet's name[280], met one of his schoolfriends[281], and were first told of and then introduced to his mentor, a hermit whose Time Lordly worldview was uncannily similar to producer Barry Letts's Buddhism[282].

Other innovations have been more radical, amending the established past rather than adding to it. *Genesis of the Daleks* itself significantly rewrites the origin story recounted in *The Daleks*

---

[276] *The Name of the Doctor, Listen.*
[277] *Hell Bent.*
[278] *The Doctor's Wife.*
[279] *Carnival of Monsters* (1973).
[280] *The Time Warrior.*
[281] *Terror of the Autons, The Sea Devils.*
[282] *The Time Monster, Planet of the Spiders.*

(1963-64); *Mawdryn Undead* (1983) places the UNIT era for the first time in the past rather than the near future; 'Escape Switch' (*The Daleks' Master Plan* episode 10, 1966) calls into question the idea that Susan named the TARDIS; and so on. One change among many – the turning of the formerly godlike Time Lords into targets of political satire in *The Deadly Assassin* – notoriously provoked the then president of the Doctor Who Appreciation Society to despair in print, 'WHAT HAS HAPPENED TO THE MAGIC OF *DOCTOR WHO?*'[283]

Yet **Doctor Who** is a drama **series**; not – or not merely – a single narrative. It must entertain and impress in the present, and its past, including the prehistoric past of the Doctor's origins, is a dramatic resource it can draw on for this purpose. It is entitled to make as free with it in the present as may be dramatically appropriate. If it seems that Moffat does this more often than most, this may be partly due to his tenure following a period in which insecurity about its viewer base made the series reluctant to reference anything more than a few years old. Whatever the predilections of individual showrunners, viewers can be certain of one thing: that **Doctor Who** – more than any other series, more even than any other 50-year-old series, not that there are very many points of comparison there – will always change.

Where other dramas have a formula, **Doctor Who** has a continuing process. Every change of lead actor is a death and resurrection. Every reintroduction of an old enemy is an upgraded emergence

---

[283] Rudzki, Jan Vincent, 'Television Review of The Deadly Assassin' (capitals Mr Rudzki's).

167

from the grave. Every reframing of a 46-year-old camera angle is an invasion of the familiar by the alien.

And every interpretation, every reading, will always be contingent – because, pending access to a real time machine, it can only take into account the context of the past, never that of the future. One day a new **Doctor Who** story – perhaps written by Moffat, perhaps by one of his successors decades from now – will provide new context or brazenly declare an outright contradiction, and *Dark Water / Death in Heaven* will change beyond recognition.

Perhaps we will learn that Clara really threw the Doctor's keys into the volcano, and everything since then has been a dream. Perhaps Missy is after all a robot, and the Master is off somewhere cackling to himself about the gullibility of his 'dear Doctor'. Perhaps the **Doctor Who** universe has a real Heaven, and Clara, Danny and Jane Austen are finally happy there together. We will only find out the new truth when it is revealed – to be overturned in its turn one day, by the hand of some later writer.

One day, everything in this book will be wrong[284]. And **that** is the magic of **Doctor Who**.

---

[284] If indeed it isn't now, which is certainly a possibility.

APPENDIX: 'YOU CAN SEE MY HOUSE FROM HERE'

All right, then. Let's finish by talking about the City of the Saved.

During the broadcast of the 2014 season, a handful of commentators on internet forums saw similarities between **Doctor Who**'s ongoing 'Promised Land' plotline and my stories set in the City of the Saved – a secular techno-utopia located beyond the end of time, where all the human dead of the **Faction Paradox** universe (originally a spinoff from the **Doctor Who** prose fiction continuum of the late 1990s) are resurrected. The rather presumptuous idea was that Steven Moffat might have borrowed a concept from an obscure series of niche-interest small-press spinoff books to canonise in the BBC's flagship drama series.

I admit there was a moment – between around 17m 37s and 17m 45s into *Dark Water* – when I actually suspected they might be right. The big reveal of the apparently infinite city of the Nethersphere – before it turned out that the point of the reveal was that said city was occupying the interior of a hollow sphere – was both thrilling and baffling, as it seemed for those few seconds that the contents of my head might somehow have found their way into broadcast **Doctor Who** without any conscious intervention on my part.

But even aside from its topology, the Nethersphere is not the City of the Saved. Its existence doesn't even contradict that of the City, for those few who still believe that the **Doctor Who** and **Faction Paradox** universes are one and the same: both are simply venues where uploaded versions of dead humans are recreated, and there could potentially be any number of those. (For similar reasons, the

169

existence of either artificial afterlife doesn't contradict the idea that their respective fictional universes might have a real one.)

The great appeal of the City (to me as an author, and I assume to the readers of *Of the City of the Saved* and Obverse Books' **City of the Saved** anthology series) is the scope for surreal juxtapositions: human beings from the past, present and future – and alternative histories – can be shown interacting together in the context of a vast metacivilisation the size of a galaxy. The potential for generating stories is enormous. There's no trace of that in Moffat's presentation of the Nethersphere: although the dead we see preceding Danny to their eternal reward include a cyborg from the past, a soldier from the future and a present-day policeman, we see no contact between them, nor indeed (as Missy is alive and Seb an AI) between any of the dead except for one pair, Danny and his victim. Aside from Seb's comment about Steve Jobs building iPads there, we get no sense of the Nethersphere's social, political or economic setup, nor of what everyday existence is like for the billions of human dead who supposedly reside in it.

Because of course none of this is what Moffat is interested in. The purposes of his afterlife are manifold – to reintroduce Missy in a role that associates her with death; to re-envisage the Cybermen as the undead; to justify the Remembrance Day imagery; to show how far the Doctor will go for Clara; to confront Danny with his guilt from the past; to allow Clara his help in dealing with the consequences of his death; to bring back the Brig – but they're dramatic functions which serve his story, not the springboard for it. Like my series, Moffat is following the Christian tradition (from which, in fact, my series takes its name) of portraying the afterlife

170

as an urban environment – but that's exactly as far as the similarities go[285].

Of course, the fact that Moffat uses one of my favourite tropes makes his story interesting to me – hence the preceding 40,000 words of this study – but no more so than Missy's gender-swap, which again pushes a lot of my imaginative buttons yet which I can hardly claim to have invented either.

To be honest, my amusement at the speculation that Moffat might have stolen the idea of the afterlife from me was coupled with a certain degree of schadenfreude. A common response to my novel *Of the City of the Saved* (2004) was that I'd obviously ripped off the idea from Philip Jose Farmer's **Riverworld** series – despite the fact that those novels are indebted to John Kendrick Bangs' **Houseboat on the Styx** books, which are clearly riffing in turn on Dante, and so on back to the *Aeneid* and beyond. It was nice not to be the one being accused of plagiarism for a change.

The Doctor tells Clara, 'Almost every culture in the universe has some concept of an afterlife,' and while we can only speculate about the universe, it's certainly true of most cultures here on Earth. The fact that earthly science fiction and fantasy authors play with the idea sometimes really doesn't mean we're cribbing from each other.

---

[285] A previous Moffat story, *Silence in the Library / Forest of the Dead*, also uses the play on meanings of the word 'saved'. But not this one.

171

BIBLIOGRAPHY

Books

Aaronovitch, Ben, *Transit*. **Doctor Who: The New Adventures**. London, Virgin Publishing Ltd, 1992. ISBN 9780426203841.

Arnold, Jon, *Rose*. **The Black Archive** #1. Edinburgh, Obverse Books, 2016. ISBN 9781909031371.

St Augustine, *City of God* (*De Civitate Dei*). 426. Henry Bettenson, trans, London, Penguin Classics, 2003. ISBN 9780140448948.

Banks, Iain M, *The Player of Games*. London, Macmillan, 1988. ISBN 9780333471104.

Baxter, Stephen, *The Wheel of Ice*. **Doctor Who**. London, BBC Books, 2012. ISBN 9781849901826.

The Bible, King James Version. 1611. Oxford, Oxford University Press, 1997. ISBN 9780192835253.

Bishop, David, *Doctor Who: Who Killed Kennedy*. London, Virgin Publishing Ltd, 1996. ISBN 9780426204671.

Bunyan, John, *The Pilgrim's Progress*. 1678. London, Penguin Classics, 2009. ISBN 9780141439716.

Cartmel, Andrew, *Cat's Cradle: Warhead*. **Doctor Who: The New Adventures**. London, Virgin Publishing Ltd, 1992. ISBN 9780426203674.

Cartmel, Andrew, *Warlock*. **Doctor Who: The New Adventures**. London, Virgin Publishing Ltd, 1995. ISBN 9780426204336.

Cartmel, Andrew, *Warchild*. **Doctor Who: The New Adventures**. London, Virgin Publishing Ltd, 1996. ISBN 9780426204640.

Conan Doyle, Arthur, *The Penguin Complete Sherlock Holmes*. 1887-1927. London, Penguin Books Ltd, 2009. ISBN 9780141040288.

The Compact Oxford English Dictionary. Second edition, 1991. ISBN 9780198612582.

Conrad, Joseph, *Heart of Darkness*. 1899. London, Penguin Classics, 2007. ISBN 9780141441672.

Cooray Smith, James, *The Massacre*. **The Black Archive** #2. Edinburgh, Obverse Books, 2016. ISBN 9781909031388.

Cornell, Paul, *Human Nature*. **Doctor Who: The New Adventures**. London, Virgin Publishing Ltd, 1995. ISBN 9780426204435.

Cornell, Paul, *Human Nature*. BBC Books edition. **Doctor Who: The History Collection**. London, Penguin Random House, 2015. ISBN 9781849909099.

Cornell, Paul, ed, *Licence Denied: Rumblings from the Doctor Who Underground*. London, Virgin Publishing Ltd, 1997. ISBN 978073501047.

Dante Alighieri, *The Divine Comedy (La Divina Commedia)*. 1320. Dorothy Sayers, trans, London, Penguin, 1949. ISBN 9780140440065, 9780140440461, 9780140441055.

Davies, Russell T, *Damaged Goods*. **Doctor Who: The New Adventures**. London, Virgin Publishing Ltd, 1996. ISBN 9780426204831.

Davies, Russell T, et al, *Doctor Who: The Shooting Scripts*. London, BBC Books, 2005. ISBN 9780563486411.

Davies, Russell T, and Benjamin Cook, *The Writer's Tale: The Final Chapter*. London, BBC Books, 2010. ISBN 9781846078613.

Delany, Samuel R, *Triton*. New York, Bantam Books, 1976. ISBN 9780553025675.

Gibson, William, *Burning Chrome and Other Stories*. 1986. London, HarperCollins, 1995. ISBN 9780006480433.

Gibson, William, *Neuromancer*. 1984. London, HarperCollins, 1993. ISBN 9780006480419.

Hickman, Clayton, ed, *Doctor Who: The Brilliant Book 2012*. London, BBC Books, 2011. ISBN 9781849902304.

Howe, David, and Stephen James Walker, *Doctor Who: The Television Companion*. London, BBC Books, 1998. ISBN 9780563405887.

Hutton, Ronald, *The Stations of the Sun: A History of the Ritual Year in Britain*. Oxford, Oxford University Press, 1996. ISBN 9780192854483.

Lane, Andy and Justin Richards, eds, *Doctor Who: Decalog 3 – Consequences*. London, Virgin Publishing Ltd, 1996. ISBN 9780426204787.

Le Guin, Ursula, *The Left Hand of Darkness*. New York, Ace Books, 1969. ISBN 9780586036419.

McAuley, Paul, *Eye of the Tyger*. **Doctor Who Novellas**. Tolworth, Telos Publishing Ltd, 2003. ISBN 9781903889244.

174

Milton, John, *Paradise Lost*. 1667. London, Penguin Classics, 2003. ISBN 9780140424393.

Purser-Hallard, Philip, *Of the City of the Saved*. **Faction Paradox**. Des Moines, Mad Norwegian Press, 2004. ISBN 9780972595940.

Reynolds, Alastair, *Harvest of Time*. **Doctor Who**. London, BBC Books, 2013. ISBN 9781849904186.

Segal, Philip, with Gary Russell, *Doctor Who: Regeneration*. London, HarperCollinsPublishers, 2000. ISBN 9780007105915.

Periodicals

Doctor Who Magazine (DWM). Marvel UK, Panini, BBC, 1979-.

Moffat, Steven, 'Production Notes'. DWM #411, cover date December 2011.

Moffat, Steven, 'Steven Moffat'. DWM #481, cover date January 2015.

'The Time Team'. DWM #490, cover date October 2015.

Gaiman, Neil. *Sandman*. Vertigo, 1989-96.

O'Mahony, Daniel, 'We Meet Again, Doctor...'. *Matrix* #48. Reprinted in Cornell, Paul, ed, *Licence Denied*, pp130-35.

Rudzki, Jan Vincent, 'Television Review of The Deadly Assassin'. *TARDIS* vol 2 #1, 1976. Reprinted in Cornell, Paul, ed, *Licence Denied*, pp3-6.

Television

An Adventure in Space and Time. BBC, 2013.

Babylon 5. Babylonian Productions Ltd, Synthetic Worlds Ltd, 1993-1998.

Blackadder Goes Forth. BBC, 1989.

Buffy the Vampire Slayer. Mutant Enemy Productions, 1997-2003.

Coupling. Hartswood Films, 2000-04.

   Nine and a Half Months, 2004.

Doctor Who. BBC, 1963-.

Doctor Who Extra. BBC, 2014-.

   Series 1 episode 11, 2014.

Elementary. CBS Television Studios, Timberman/Beverly Productions, Hill of Beans Productions, 2012-.

Firefly. Mutant Enemy Productions, 20th Century Fox Television, 2002.

K-9 and Company. BBC, 1981.

   A Girl's Best Friend.

Red Dwarf. Grant Naylor, Baby Cow Productions, 1988-99, 2009, 2012-.

   Future Echoes, 1988.

The Sarah Jane Adventures. BBC, 2007-11.

   Enemy of the Bane, 2008.

Sherlock. Hartswood Films, BBC Wales, WGBH, 2010-.

Star Trek: Deep Space Nine. Paramount Domestic Television, 1993-99.

176

Star Trek: The Next Generation. Paramount Domestic Television, 1987-94.

Torchwood. BBC Wales, BBC Worldwide, Canadian Broadcasting Corporation, Starz Entertainment, 2006-11.

Everything Changes, 2006.

Cyberwoman, 2006.

They Keep Killing Suzie, 2006.

Random Shoes, 2006.

The X-Files. Ten Thirteen Productions, 20th Television, 20th Century Fox Television, 1993-2002, 2016.

Film

Myth Makers: Jon Pertwee. Reeltime Pictures, 1989.

Attenborough, Richard, dir, *Oh! What a Lovely War*. Accord Productions, 1969.

Barnfather, Keith, dir, *Dæmos Rising*. Reeltime Pictures, 2004.

Barnfather, Keith, and Christopher Barry, dirs, *Downtime*. Dominitemporal Services, Reeltime Pictures, Tropicana Holdings, 1995.

Mayo, Archie, dir, *Night after Night*. Paramount Pictures, 1932.

Salles, Walter, dir, *Dark Water*. Touchstone Pictures, 2005.

Sax, Geoffrey, dir, *White Noise*. Universal Pictures et al, 2005.

Scott, Ridley, dir, *Blade Runner*. The Ladd Company, Shaw Brothers, Warner Bros, Blade Runner Partnership, 1982.

Web

'Manic Pixie Dream Girl.' TV Tropes. http://tvtropes.org/pmwiki/pmwiki.php/Main/ManicPixieDreamGi rl. Accessed 18 December 2015.

'Manipulative boyfriends vote Danny Pink best **Doctor Who** companion'. *The Daily Mash*, 28 October 2014. http://www.thedailymash.co.uk/news/arts-entertainment/manipulative-boyfriends-vote-danny-pink-best-doctor-who-companion-2014102892170. Accessed 18 December 2015.

'Poems and Poets of the First World War.' The Great War 1914-1918. http://www.greatwar.co.uk/poems/.

> Binyon, Lawrence, 'For the Fallen'. http://www.greatwar.co.uk/poems/laurence-binyon-for-the-fallen.htm. Accessed 18 December 2015.

> McCrae, John, 'In Flanders Fields'. http://www.greatwar.co.uk/poems/john-mccrae-in-flanders-fields.htm. Accessed 18 December 2015.

> 'Inspiration for the poem 'In Flanders Fields' by John McCrae'. http://www.greatwar.co.uk/poems/john-mccrae-in-flanders-fields-inspiration.htm. Accessed 18 December 2015.

'White Poppy for a Culture of Peace'. Peace Pledge Union. http://www.ppu.org.uk/whitepoppy/index.html. Accessed 18 December 2015.

Burns, Stuart Ian, 'Death in Heaven'. *Feeling Listless*, 8 November 2014. http://feelinglistless.blogspot.co.uk/2014/11/death-in-heaven.html. Accessed 18 December 2015.

Clarke, Gavin, 'Doctor Who Trashing the TARDIS, Clara Alone, Useless UNIT: *Death in Heaven*'. *The Register*, 8 November 2014. http://www.theregister.co.uk/2014/11/08/doctor_who_death_in_heaven_review_episode_12/. Accessed 18 December 2015.

Clute, John, and David Langford, eds, *The Encyclopedia of Science Fiction*. http://www.sf-encyclopedia.com/.

> Langford, David, and Brian M Stableford, 'Upload'. 22 April 2015. http://www.sf-encyclopedia.com/entry/upload. Accessed 18 December 2015.

> Nicholls, Peter, 'Cyberpunk'. 10 April 2015. http://www.sf-encyclopedia.com/entry/cyberpunk. Accessed 18 December 2015.

> Nicholls, Peter, and David Langford, 'Steampunk'. 22 April 2015. http://www.sf-encyclopedia.com/entry/steampunk. Accessed 18 December 2015.

Foxton, Willard, 'The Loathsome Britain First Are Trying to Hijack The Poppy – Don't Let Them'. *The Telegraph*, 4 November 2014. http://www.telegraph.co.uk/history/world-war-one/11207973/The-loathsome-Britain-First-are-trying-to-hijack-the-poppy-dont-let-them.html. Accessed 18 December 2015.

Gaiman, Neil, 'A Fairly Humongous **Doctor Who** Q&A Mostly'. Journal, 9 June 2011. http://journal.neilgaiman.com/2011/06/fairly-humongous-doctor-who-q-mostly.html. Accessed 18 December 2015.

179

Graham, Jack, 'Sex, Death & Rock 'n' Roll'. *Shabogan Graffiti*, 30 September 2010. http://shabogangraffiti.blogspot.co.uk/2010/09/sex-death-rock-n-roll.html. Accessed 18 December 2015.

Greenslade, Roy, 'Rightwing Press Mounts Assault over Jeremy Corbyn's Cenotaph Nod'. *The Guardian*, 9 November 2015. http://www.theguardian.com/media/greenslade/2015/nov/09/jeremy-corbyn-suffers-yet-another-round-of-negative-headlines. Accessed 18 December 2015.

Harness, Peter, Twitter conversation. 4 September 2015. https://twitter.com/mrpeterharness/status/639775580163018752. Accessed 18 December 2015.

Holmes, Jonathan, 'Doctor Who: Who Is Missy?'. *Radio Times*, 23 August 2014. http://www.radiotimes.com/news/2014-08-23/doctor-who-who-is-missy. Accessed 18 December 2015. Accessed 18 December 2015.

Kerry, Michelle, 'Little Boxes Will Make You Angry: **Doctor Who** and Transphobia'. *Doctor Who TV*, 27 January 2015. http://www.doctorwhotv.co.uk/little-boxes-will-make-you-angry-doctor-who-and-transphobia-71391.htm. Accessed 18 December 2015.

Lillemose, Jacob and Matthias Kryger, 'The (Re)invention of Cyberspace'. *Kunstkritikk*, 28 August 2015. http://www.kunstkritikk.com/kommentar/the-reinvention-of-cyberspace/. Accessed 18 December 2015.

Martin, Dan, 'Doctor Who: Asylum of the Daleks – spoiler-free review'. *The Guardian*, 15 August 2012.

http://www.theguardian.com/tv-and-radio/tvandradioblog/2012/aug/15/doctor-who-asylum-of-the-daleks. Accessed 18 December 2015.

Martin, Dan, 'Doctor Who recap: Series 34, episode 9 – *Flatline*'. *The Guardian*, 18 October 2014. http://www.theguardian.com/tv-and-radio/2014/oct/18/doctor-who-recap-series-34-episode-9-flatline. Accessed 18 December 2015.

Spangenberg, Lisa L, 'Did the Celts or Druids Perform Human Sacrifice?'. *Celtic Studies Resources*. http://www.digitalmedievalist.com/opinionated-celtic-faqs/human-sacrifice/. Accessed 18 December 2015.

Tweedy, Rod, 'My Name Is Legion – The British Legion and the Control of Remembrance'. Veterans for Peace, 5 November 2015. http://veteransforpeace.org.uk/2015/my-name-is-legion/. Accessed 18 December 2015.

Wiggins, Anna, 'Regeneration: A Personal History of Doctor Who'. Eruditorium Press, January 2015. http://www.philipsandifer.com/blog/regeneration-a-personal-history-of-doctor-who/. Accessed 18 December 2015.

Wilkins, Alasdair, 'Doctor Who: Death in Heaven'. AV Club, 8 November 2014. www.avclub.com/tvclub/doctor-who-death-heaven-211601. Accessed 18 December 2015.

BIOGRAPHY

Black Archive series editor **Philip Purser-Hallard** gained his Oxford doctorate in English Literature with a thesis on 'The Relationship between Creator and Creature in Science Fiction'.

He is the author of the urban fantasy thriller trilogy **The Devices** – *The Pendragon Protocol* (2014), *The Locksley Exploit* (2015) and *Trojans* (2016) – about a war between present-day avatars of King Arthur and Robin Hood. His other published fiction includes two **Doctor Who** short stories and one featuring Sherlock Holmes, and stories and novellas occupying many of the more distant niches on the family tree of **Doctor Who** spinoffs.

He edits the **City of the Saved** short story anthologies for Obverse Books, set in the techno-utopian afterlife of his novel *Of the City of the Saved* (2004), and also edited the Obverse Books anthology *Iris Wildthyme of Mars* (2014). The British Fantasy Society described him as 'the best-kept secret in British genre writing.'